Praise for *Me and My Mentor*

'Everyone can read or listen to wise people passing down truisms; the difficulty is that none are directly relevant and often frustratingly obscure. Mentors breathe life into how to go forward explaining the relevance to the particular situation and to the individual traits of the mentee. At their very best mentors inspire with words that resonate for years to come. This book is an excellent guide for both mentors and mentees. Norah has assembled the very best of the best and set questions from their experiences for all of us to ponder. In doing so, she has opened the door on these relationships and called us in.'

— Nerida Wallace, CEO, Law Institute of Victoria

'Among the plethora of books on mentoring, Norah Breekveldt's Me and My Mentor *stands out because of the diversity in the mentoring relationships described through the stories of each mentor and mentee. In my view, there is no one 'right way', no set formula, to mentor or be mentored—and the stories generously shared in this book illustrate this beautifully.'*

— Dr. Niki Vincent, South Australian Commissioner for Equal Opportunity

'Insightful and entertaining, this book provides guidance on how to engage in a successful mentoring relationship. Great leaders develop and nurture other people. The stories in this book will inspire you to go ahead and enter into a mentoring relationship.'

— Mary-Jane Ierodiaconou, Honourable Associate Justice of the Supreme Court of Victoria

Me and My Mentor

Me and My Mentor

How mentoring supercharged the careers of 11 extraordinary women

Norah Breekveldt

with *Emma Russell*

M
MELBOURNE BOOKS

Published by Melbourne Books
Level 9, 100 Collins Street,
Melbourne, VIC 3000
Australia
www.melbournebooks.com.au
info@melbournebooks.com.au

Title: Me and My Mentor: How mentoring supercharged the careers of 11 extraordinary women
Author: Norah Breekveldt with Emma Russell
ISBN: 9781925556230

A catalogue record for this book is available from the National Library of Australia

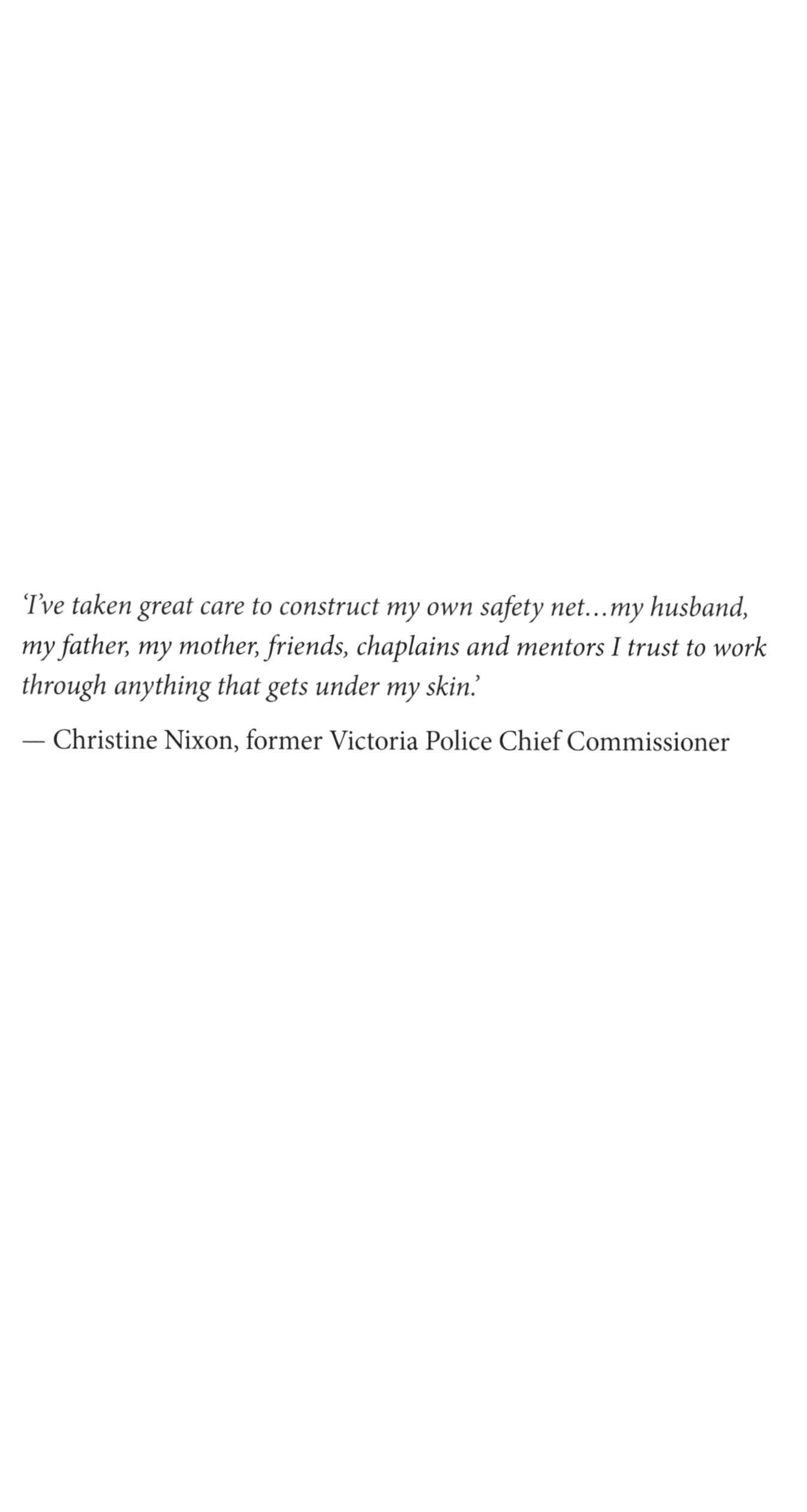

'I've taken great care to construct my own safety net…my husband, my father, my mother, friends, chaplains and mentors I trust to work through anything that gets under my skin.'

— Christine Nixon, former Victoria Police Chief Commissioner

Contents

Dr. Niki Vincent

South Australian Commissioner for Equal Opportunity

Preface

While the intensity of interest, research and books about mentoring is a relatively recent phenomenon (that continues to grow in momentum) mentoring relationships appear to have been an integral part of many cultures for thousands of years[1]. This, in itself, is testament to their value and impact.

Among the plethora of books on mentoring, Norah Breekveldt's *Me and My Mentor* stands out because of the diversity in the mentoring relationships described through the stories of each mentor and mentee. In my view, there is no one 'right way', no set formula, to mentor or be mentored—and the stories generously shared in this book illustrate this beautifully.

Throughout my career, I've had (and still have) many formal and informal mentors. I've also formally and informally mentored many people. Like those described within the pages ahead, each of my mentoring relationships has been different—organically tailored to the personalities, skills, experience, expertise, goals and available time of the people involved. Some relationships have been very long, and some have been short-term, with a very specific purpose or goal to orient them. There is not a story in this book that didn't resonate with my experience in many ways—and that I didn't learn something very useful from.

My own mentors have included some of my former bosses, board members, an academic supervisor and colleagues—almost all of whom, interestingly, have been men. There is no doubt that each of these relationships have made a great difference in my life. My mentors have supported my confidence and courage at times when these were wavering, they have provided sounding boards for difficult decisions, advice about unfamiliar situations encountered in roles in new sectors, and confirmation, constructive criticism and alternative perspectives when I've needed these. Each of my mentors has also told me how much they've grown and learned from our relationship. Mentoring should be a mutually beneficial experience.

I've had many mentees in the past—both women and men. I currently mentor several young women, including a fifteen-year-old Liberian immigrant from an underprivileged background, and I'm an informal mentor for many of the members of my current team. In alignment with several of the titles of the chapters in this book, I feel I've helped mentees to push boundaries, find their voice and nurture their passions—and I hope that each one of them has felt that I've 'had their back'. The reciprocity from these relationships has been amazing. I've learned so much from every one of my mentees, and felt privileged to be able to contribute to their development.

In her introduction to this book, Norah Breekveldt has noted that although the insights from the stories in this book are applicable to all adults, women have a special need to be mentored because of the inequities that remain in the workforce.

We know that whilst important progress has been made on this front, there is sadly still a very long way to go. We have a stark underrepresentation of women in our state and federal parliaments, eight ASX200 company boards still do not have any women members and only eleven have a woman chief executive. The latest statistics show that the gender pay gap is still massive—and this translates into similarly massive average earnings and superannuation deficits over a lifetime. These deficits are even higher for those with university degrees (with average graduate starting salaries for women being five percent less than their male peers in the same industry).

At the heart of the gender pay gap is the definition of merit—and the fact that the work women do is not as valued as the work that men do (even if it's the same work!). I really appreciated Our Watch's recent short video[2] which shows how beliefs and behaviours that reflect disrespect for girls and women and reinforce stereotypical gender roles, relations and identities are part of most children's lives from the get-go—and they impact both females and males. These stereotypes not only impact how the work that women do is valued, they also mean that although we've seen a massive shift of women into paid work, we've seen no real shift in the opposite direction. This, as Annabel Crabb has pointed out[3], means that women frequently combine their careers with a second shift when they get home. As Crabb noted 'We won't fix the work problem until we fix the home problem.' While successful women are frequently asked about how they juggle work and family, we need to start asking this of men too. It makes no sense to me that a lack of childcare is a drain on women's careers and yet there is no evidence that it's holding back men's careers in any way. The sad fact is that if it was, it would likely have been fixed decades ago.

Reputable study after reputable study shows that there are sound economic reasons why gender inequality should be addressed. This won't happen if we simply use our mentoring to help women fit better into organisations that were designed for men in traditional gender roles.

I hope I've been able to help my female and male mentees (and some of my mentors) challenge some of the tenacious gender stereotypes that limit both women and men. For me, it's been particularly important that I don't just help my mentees fit better into organisations and systems that perpetuate inequality—but that

I help them become aware of these issues and change them. This is because, as author Catherine Fox said recently '… no amount of leaning in will break down the old boys club or narrow the gender pay gap.'[4]

We need to use mentoring to empower a redesign of organisational structures and cultures so that everyone will have an equal chance to contribute both at home and in the workplace. I've enjoyed reading about how so many of the mentoring relationships in this book were about (or involved elements of) doing just that!

1 www.us.corwin.com/sites/default/files/upm-binaries/17419_Chapter_1.pdf
2 www.youtube.com/watch?v=fLUVWZvVZXw
3 The Wife Drought by Annabel Crabb, Ebury Press, 2014
4 The Australian, 'Why it's time to stop fixing women' Catherine Fox

Norah Breekveldt

Norah is a leadership coach and consultant. She supports business leaders dedicated to advancing gender equity and diversity in their workplaces, and empowers women to lead with confidence and create successful careers.

Norah began her career in the public sector, then progressed into senior executive roles in the corporate world. As one of the few women on senior executive teams, she understands the dynamics of creating lasting change in complex, traditional organisations.

She is the recipient of the BCA/AFR Work and Family Award in 1993 for the introduction of work and family practices at Kemcor, and a Telstra Business Women's Award in 1995.

Norah is the author of *Sideways To The Top – 10 Stories of Successful Women That Will Change Your Thinking About Careers Forever* (Melbourne Books, 2013) and *Career Interrupted – How 14 Successful Women Navigate Career Breaks* (Melbourne Books, 2015).

Introduction

'I think the key is for women not to set any limits.'
— Martina Navratilova, former world number 1 tennis player.

Kate found it challenging returning to work from maternity leave, and would have felt satisfied returning to a job in her comfort zone. She said if it weren't for her mentor Adam challenging her thinking she could have missed out on taking one of the best jobs she's ever had.

As Sophie's mentor, Jodi has been her greatest cheerleader as well as her toughest critic. Jodi reminds other women to be kind and generous to those coming up behind them and to remember how tough it was when they were younger and striving to succeed.

Wayne believes he is a better football coach and a more mature, grounded and balanced person from having coached women and having a female mentor, Chyloe.

Bec was sixteen years old when she first met Jerril and got a glimpse of what life as a performing artist could be. Jerril knew she had found a kindred spirit in Bec and committed herself to guiding

Bec through the difficult professional decisions and life choices a performing artist must inevitably make.

These are just a few of the stories explored in *Me and My Mentor*, some of them never before told. The experiences and reflections of these women move our thinking beyond descriptions of theory and best practice. They reveal stories of real-life experiences with the voices of women whose mentors were a constant source of inspiration, personal growth and perspective.

Changing hearts and minds one story at a time

The lessons and insights contained in these stories can be applied to both men and women, yet women have a special need to be mentored because of the inequities they continue to experience in the workplace. While women continue to outperform men educationally and are more likely to complete tertiary studies than men[1] the leadership gap stubbornly remains. The pipeline of women into management roles is strengthening, yet women continue to be under-represented at the top, with five out of every six CEO roles still being held by men.[2] Just as disappointingly, the pay gap has been hovering at between fifteen percent and nineteen percent over the last two decades, but increasing towards management level and reaching 28.8 percent for managers[3]. Mentoring is one way to start changing these numbers.

What is mentoring?

Textbook definitions often describe mentoring as a professional relationship between an older, wiser, senior mentor sharing their work experiences and wisdom with a younger, junior and inexperienced mentee. This concept has its roots in Greek mythology, when Odysseus, commencing his journey to Troy, entrusted his house and his son's education to his friend, Mentor. 'Tell him all you know,' Odysseus said, and from then the definition of mentoring was firmly established.

However, the real-life experiences of mentors and mentees interviewed in this study demonstrate that the practice of mentoring has moved beyond this top-down construct of a great philosopher or teacher imparting wisdom to a protégé. Mentoring is an evolving process, often with shifting boundaries and changing landscapes. The stories in this book show there is no single definition for a mentor and mentee relationship.

Perhaps it is time to broaden the definition of mentoring and put aside unhelpful and restrictive boundaries. David Kay and Roger Hinds come close when they describe mentoring simply as 'one person helping another to achieve something…that is important to them.'[4] The experiences of women in our research do just that—they demonstrate the many faces of mentoring, with each relationship finding its own meaning, purpose and process. However I also love the simplicity of Oprah Winfrey's description of mentoring that 'A mentor is someone who allows you to see the hope inside yourself.' The experiences of women in our research demonstrate all of these traits—they inspire hope, plus theydemonstrate the many faces of mentoring, with each relationship finding its own meaning, purpose and process.

The role of mentoring in women's careers

There are many barriers that explain the ongoing lack of women's career success just as there are many strategies women can adopt to overcome these barriers. Mentoring is important but in the end is just one of these strategies.

Reflecting on the stories of success described in the following chapters helps us better understand how women can maximise mentoring opportunities as one critical development and promotion strategy amongst several.

Rethinking what you know about mentoring

As a woman navigating the complexities of the workplace, I encourage you to be inspired by the journeys and the remarkable stories profiled in this book. Perhaps you will be able to personally relate to some of their 'sliding door' moments and begin to understand how they felt when they worked through seemingly impossible problems and situations, and found the best possible outcome.

If you are a leader or senior decision-maker, these stories are offered to help you understand how practical leadership can make a real difference in the career development of talented women.

If you are a mentor, you are invited to learn from the journeys described and the experiences of other mentors and apply it to your own mentoring journey.

To all the readers of this book, I hope you will find much value in these stories and gain valuable insights that you can apply to your own career journey.

1 www.wgea.gov.au/sites/default/files/gender-pay-gap-statistics.pdf
2 www.wgea.gov.au/media-releases/australia's-latest-gender-equality-scorecard-released
3 Ibid p. 60
4 D. Kay & R. Hinds, A Practical Guide to Mentoring, second edition, 2005, How to Books Ltd., p. IX

The Eleven Stories

'One of the things I am good at as an institute director is being generous. And that means being generous with your time. Taking time out to mentor our young Aboriginal researchers is really important, taking time to find out about what is happening to people in the Institute and where they are going - it takes time to be generous...'

— Professor Fiona Stanley, 2010 Australian of the Year

'Try and swim, try and swim. Don't sink'

◇◇◇◇◇

Pat McCabe & Michelle Britbart

Retired law firm partner and QC

Pat McCabe

Pat McCabe has recently retired after fifty-six years as an insurance lawyer based in Melbourne. Pat's legal career spans common law, litigation and commercial fraud, major government inquiries and royal commissions. He was a co-author of the 'bottom of the harbour' taxation investigation report in 1982. He is highly respected for his grasp of statutory common law rules and procedures and state and federal governments regularly sought his advice throughout his career.

Pat had a long-standing interest in insurance and personal injury litigation. He advised the Victorian government in relation to serious injury policy in respect to the restoration of common law rights for seriously injured workers and on policy issues arising under the tort reforms and the implementation of the reforms in the *Wrongs Act* (VIC 1958). He was also responsible for overseeing the drafting and introduction of significant legislation in the areas of accident and injury claims, including the serious injury provisions of the *Accident Compensation Act* and the second reading speech for the reintroduction of common law rights.

Michelle Britbart

Michelle Britbart has been a barrister at the Victorian Bar since 2004. Before that she spent nine years as a solicitor, mainly working in personal injuries and government litigation at Dunhill Madden Butler. She was appointed Queen's Counsel in 2015. Michelle's main areas of practice are common law jury trials in the areas of public liability litigation, personal injuries and other medico-legal matters. She undertook a Master's in Health and Medical Law at Melbourne University and holds a Graduate Diploma in Genetic Counselling from Murdoch Children's Research Institute and the University of Melbourne.

Pat's story

My journey has been one that doesn't have many comparatives. I did my degree part time working in the state Crown Solicitor's office and then the Parliamentary draftsman office, went to the bar, left and became a senior partner in a major law firm, in the course of which, due to a conflict of interest issue in the firm, I became a sole practitioner for a time before returning. That breadth of experience gave me an appreciation of the different skill sets required in each area of practice.

The snuffbox of power

I spent my first ten years in the Crown. I firstly worked in the criminal law branch, instructing the prosecutors—including Bidstrup, Moloney, Mullally, Moore and Byrne—in the criminal courts of general sessions, now the County Court. Each day I would witness the best criminal lawyers arguing the principles of evidence. It was inspiring to see the great names—Cullity QC, Gillespie-Jones QC, Galbally, Dunn, Walker, Bryson, Reid and Gray—in action. The one setback was that the position did not permit attendance at lectures. One day in 1965 John Finemore QC, the Parliamentary Counsel, invited me to his office. He opened, 'I just want to inform you that your record is the worst of all the part time lawyers in the crown. But what it reveals is that you've been out after dark, and that's the role. So I'm going to nominate you for Secretary of the Standing Committee of Commonwealth and States Attorneys.' He elaborated that Attorney General Sir Arthur Rylah was keen to control the agenda of the committee and prevent a takeover by the triangle of power in Canberra. The Committee was what I call the snuffbox of power, where law and politics collided. It was an enormously dynamic group including all the attorneys, their senior officers, and officers of the states. It was responsible for the creation of the *Uniform Companies Acts* and the Petroleum OffShore Lands legislation. From time to time I'd be requested to draft bills for the committee. I drafted Australia's first privacy bill, the *Listening Devices Act*.

I completed my articles under the Crown Solicitor in the Common Law. The white ribbon briefs where only delivered to the those who where eminent and highly ethical in the fairness of presentation of the Crown case.I was able to instruct counsel such as Jack Winneke and Stephen Charles whose later achievements underline my good fortune in being able to learn from them.

I decided I would go to the bar from there, but a call from Rob Elder of Madden Butler and Graham, the predecessor firm of Dunhill Madden Butler, persuaded me to join the firm in the insurance group. As most litigation involves insurance I recognised the offer was an opportunity. Four years later I finally got to the bar and had the privilege of reading with two of the most eminent common law counsel in Sher QC, who took silk whilst I was his reader, and then Stanley QC. I was at the bar for eight years and authored the highly controversial McCabe-La Franchi 'bottom of the harbour' report into tax evasion (1982). The findings of that report and the Costigan report created a public and political furore about tax evasion. The profile wasn't comfortable for me—there were threats to La Franchi and myself. Dunhill Madden Butler then offered me a partnership, I thought 'why not, it's a safe place out of the spotlight I'll go back there for five years.' Ultimately five years stretched to thirty-five years, with a brief gap in the middle when I set up my own firm, McCabe's. This was necessary as I was acting for a person of interest in the Ambulance Services Royal Commission in 2000, when my firm merged with Deacons who were the solicitors to the Royal Commission. I came back to Deacons as a partner at the conclusion of the commission in 2003.

My work focus changed to delivery of litigation services to the Victorian Government and medical defence.I retired as a partner in 2009 and continued as a consultant to the government on the Bushfires Royal Commission and then assisted Nicole Wearne and

Abigail McGregor in the defence of the claims against the State. Finally retiring in 2016 after a fifty-four-year career that created a truly rewarding life enriched by a legacy of friendships such Michelle.

Moments that changed me

John Finemore QC influenced me more than anyone else. He was a superlative draftsman and a brilliant lawyer. During his time 4600 bills were passed. He strongly believed in providing greater opportunities for women in the law. He ignored the barriers to married women being appointed permanent public servants and employed women lawyers even though they were banned in the Crown Solicitors office and unknown in other parts of the public service. He was years ahead of his time. John regarded women as superior in abstract reasoning and to be trusted to deliver. Women had the strength of mind to accept the greatest challenges in the law: drafting legislation; being in the parliament; able to adapt and make amendments as necessary and see through the business of the government of the day. He proudly proclaimed the intellect of women with these abilities provided security of good laws for the state. During my time in the Parliamentary Counsel's office, John brought in Jan Wade, who later became Attorney General, Rowena Armstrong QC who later succeeded John as Parliamentary Counsel and the present Chief Justice of the Supreme Court Marilyn Warren, amongst others.

> *One of the reflections of my early career was that there was no such thing as structured mentoring. Often I had to work out by myself whatever the purpose was and create a pathway to get it done.*

And time was of the essence. So energy levels were demanded which are normally not required in every job. When Finemore instructed me to create the first privacy bill in Australia there were no drafting instructions. Rather it was research English and American legislation and draft a bill for the committee to debate. Another example was when Sir Daryl Dawson QC, our Solicitor General, and Haddon Storey, the Attorney General, met with me in relation to the appointment as an investigator into the 'bottom of the harbour' schemes. I said 'where do I start?' and Sir Daryl replied, 'with a blank sheet of knowledge'. The absence of structured mentoring was such that at times in my career I felt I was running matters about which I was totally inexperienced. I can remember running a *Wrongs Act* claim in 1970 without knowing how to assess a *Wrongs Act* claim. I learned by trial and error and bluff. I hope I passed on the importance of self-confidence and bluff in my mentoring. Building self-confidence in your lawyers and being able to commence your letter of advice with 'In my opinion'; that's the thing. You've got to develop the confidence that comes with a positive mindset and believing that we are all equal in and before the law. And that was clearly something I learned from being in the Crown where I could go down the corridor at the same time as the Deputy Premier and the Attorney or Solicitor General. As a result, I would always assert to my young lawyers that they should never be overawed by any opponent.

Building a team of fearless advocates

I had one rule in life—to give to my team members what I would have hoped to have had at the same time in my career. Young lawyers often have a fear or under-assessment of their own skill set or potential. But they need to see themselves as equals with older practitioners and have a go. Having been at the bar it was always foremost in my mind that every member of my team would have the capacity to appear in court, and develop the confidence to address the court and deal with whatever the other party is going to raise. And eighty percent of what the other party was going to raise would not be contained in their affidavit of support. So you've got to be well prepared and intuitive in your ability to respond on your feet.

Frankly, insurance law is a 'non-sexy' area. It is not the kind of practice where you could go home to your family and say 'I'm doing the next big commercial deal and Freehills are opposed to me!' So I had to make 'working with Pat' something that was attractive. If you say 'insurance' it sounds boring but we were dealing with people and acting for the Transport Accident Commission or the VWA. We developed a strong ethical standard that became recognised and well regarded. I wanted to be seen as leading a group who were regarded by their opponents as fair but hard and be rated by the client as the best service providers on the panel. Part of my hyperbole was to say, 'work with me for a year and I will make you a lawyer with at least three to five years' experience at the end of it. You will be able to leave me and go out into any other field of litigation and be immediately competent to a level of seventy percent, you will then have the chance to pick up the other fifteen percent'. None of us get beyond that.

Altered states of mind

The 1980s was an era when diversity was all of a sudden no longer the elephant in the room. People were asking 'how can we get women into the partnership?' In the '90s we had a young chief executive partner in David Nathan. David wanted a firm with people who had had exposure to life outside the law, and he wanted more women in the firm. But frankly, there were some people in the firm who initially found it hard to work with a woman. Human Resources would ring me and ask, 'Pat can I send someone down to you?' And they'd arrive with a Kleenex box. I think we had to have two in a room for a while because I had so many in the team. And it was in an era when the TAC would give me as much work as I could handle, so that was great.

There were a few barristers who also had difficulty accepting women instructing in matters. They would say things like 'I don't want to deal with you', 'get Pat up here.' I even wrote two letters to different silks informing them that their conduct was inappropriate, and if I had another report about them I would inform the bar council.

That worked. How to manage your counsel is an art, particularly when settlement offer and counter offer are not far apart. I instilled into the team that the instructing solicitor, no matter their level of experience, is the most important part of the process in court, they're the ones who give instructions to counsel, not take instructions from counsel, and any developments in instructions were made by the solicitor consequential upon making a recommendation to the client.

McCabe's wisdom

I regarded annual performance reviews as a sterile process. I preferred personal bi-monthly coffees, lunches or whatever with each member of the team; I'd take them out of the office and we'd sit down and enjoy the moment. I understood about people's need for diversity or part-time work or trying new things. I had someone who wanted to be a stand-up comedian for two days a week, and someone else who was an author and producer of plays. So I would help where I could to enable them to combine their hobby and their career. Likewise, with women requiring flexible hours or days. The ideal was to achieve the best outcome and realise potential in all endeavours. I would tell the team that I understood that all of them would one day leave but that did not alter my regard for them or my willingness to help them. Otherwise anyone who wanted my chair was free to apply—they just had to beat me to the desk at 6am.

I can remember having a lunch with Michelle and saying, 'Tontini-Filippini is the only ethicist in the state, and he presents a very Catholic view on all ethical matters. I see you as having the potential to develop a role in ethics, and you could be the next go-to ethicist lawyer in this state. So I want you to push by getting into the medical field,' where the big ethical issues were.

I used Sir Daryl Dawson's 'blank sheet of knowledge' philosophy, and I also had other phrases I used, like 'bare desk energy'. That means you can get energy out of a bare desk, because it's there to be filled. In other words, you should never be afraid of not having any work.

It creates some momentum; people will find you and realise you're available. Another is 'going into a tunnel where there's no light at all' and 'finding a pathway to use your ideas'. These were strategies to deal with the need to be positive no matter. As mentor you've got to be able to develop those notions as part of building confidence. Even in the face of superior court precedent I would say, unless it is a decision of the High Court, find a point of difference. I had no involvement in Michelle's plans to join the bar but I remember telling her 'I expect you to apply. To be a leader for women it's very important that you take the next step.'

I think mentoring as understood today is more a management tool of this century, just as leading and managing people was the phrase for the last century. This century there is an expectation that a mentor will provide a structured process. My approach was more tilted to the deep end experience with support. In my group I had cells led by members with expertise in particular fields, for example, medical or the AMA guides, drafting and VCAT. The team rotated and were then given active roles in preparation of advices and appearances in court at directions hearings and at conferences. They would then be thrown in the deep end with my assurance that I would be holding them by the hair and never let them drown. There is an enormous gap between someone being a very competent student with a great degree, and being successful in practice, so it's an extraordinary privilege being their mentor; to be presented with a lot of plastic and putty, and effectively create the pillars for their careers and love of the law.

Although it was a privilege to be a mentor, I also did it because I had a personal advantage in being able to build a team who were loyal and were fantastic in the way they delivered their advices. When you come into a law firm it's not good to learn by happenstance and working it out. You've got to be smarter than that in managing your people. We built a consciousness about how to think outside the square and to be productive both as individuals and as team members and enjoy and have fun as part of the team. And yes, celebrating our victories was done robustly. There were fourteen in my TAC team and thirty-six in my VWA team.

Building empowerment means there's a lot of personal trust both ways. But when you go to the bar you've got to develop a relationship in that sphere, and likewise when you go to another firm, even though I've built you to go to another firm, if you're opposed to me, yeah, look out!

Michelle's story

I met Pat while I was still at law school. I completed a summer clerkship at Dunhill Madden Butler and I spent some time in the group that Pat headed. The following year I started working for Pat as an articled clerk. He was really my first contact with what the law is about and how the law is practiced, and working with him set the scene for where things were going to go.

Try and swim, don't sink ...

> *Our mentoring relationship evolved naturally. I think mentoring, for a lot of high achieving people, can be about their own egos. For Pat it never was.*

The importance of hierarchy in some law firms can mean young lawyers really underestimate themselves, as Pat said. He was different because he believed in us and trusted us to achieve, whilst always being there in the background to pick up the pieces if something went wrong or to gently direct us towards the right answer. And that was huge. For instance, I'd been in the group for about a month and one of the first year solicitors was leaving to travel for twelve months. Pat walked me into the solicitor's office and said 'there you go, that's all yours now.' I didn't know where to start or what to do. My head was spinning. But it was the most enormous vote of confidence. And I knew he was there if I needed help. But a lot of it is 'try and swim, try and swim, don't sink'.

Pat always encouraged us to trust our instincts. He would say 'put your opinion at the front of the letter and don't be scared to have an opinion. You might have an opinion that other people don't agree with, but that's your well thought-out opinion and you have to state it'. Of course, it had to be predicated on having a brain and doing the work, but that's not enough. We were always encouraged to do our own appearance work to the extent that it was appropriate as a solicitor. Get up, do it, have a go.

I remember early on in my time at Dunhill Madden Butler we had a client who was being interviewed by the police in a high profile matter, and the interview had to be conducted on a day that Pat was leaving the country. He left me in charge of getting the client through the interview. I was incredibly nervous, but ringing in my ears was the question 'what would Pat do now?' Luckily we'd had enough time together for me to identify those things, but that question was always the guiding light if I ever felt out of my depth. I think I did a good job, although he always managed to carry himself with a lot more ease and humour than I did in those days.

'Tell him I sent you'

I think this was unusual at the time, but Pat made absolutely no distinction amongst his solicitors based on gender; it was irrelevant to him. If anything he was very supportive when I went off and had children, and accommodated part-time work when I was ready to come back. He had a complete commitment to having the job done well by people who are good at it, rather than any other consideration.

That wasn't true of everyone. The first couple of times a [male] barrister refused to speak to us as [female] instructing solicitors we'd go back with our eyes all shiny and tears about to pop and say 'Pat he asked for you, he won't talk to me.' And Pat would say 'no, off you go. Tell him I sent you.' With the knowledge that Pat trusted us to handle the situation came a growing belief that we actually could. But he did also step in behind the scenes afterwards and say 'we won't be briefing people again who don't behave appropriately to my solicitors.'

'Play where the ball isn't'

Our work involved looking at a lot of medical issues, which I had become interested in. Pat would notice any interest that each of us had and would push us in that direction, so he encouraged me to study bio-ethics at the University of Melbourne. He also encouraged us to work hard and play hard, that was a huge emphasis. He had a lot of phrases and one I remember was 'play where the ball isn't'. He encouraged us to look other than where everyone else was looking, for the answer to it, or from another angle on the problem, or another direction for the case to take.

Our working relationship was like a constant dialogue about things and it had a huge impact on my decision to go to the bar. We'd always been encouraged to do our own advocacy, and advocacy was always presented as being a very important part of your skill set as a solicitor. We were encouraged to go up to chambers, to express our opinions to barristers and to be part of the conversation, so that confidence was there to think well you know, we can do this. When I decided to go to the bar, Pat was enormously supportive, more than I could have imagined given that I was leaving the firm. He took me out to lunch and said 'right let's talk about which clerks you might want to apply to.' We talked about what I wanted or needed and he'd done some research to find out who would be the best match for me. He organised the firm to buy me my barristerial robes, and he bought me my barristerial jacket. Those gestures showed an enormous loyalty that extended well beyond the boundaries of work.

When I got to the bar a lot of the lessons I learnt from Pat helped me have an opinion and be involved. That meant when I was even a very junior barrister, I always thought I had a seat at the table. So without being pushy about it, a lot of the QCs I would be junior to said they found it very hard to shake me off when they were negotiating with their opponents, because I would always be there listening to understand how it worked. I felt the confidence and entitlement to do that because I'd been given that confidence every day working as a solicitor in Pat's team.

When I went to the bar I managed not working with Pat very badly I think. There was a long time when we didn't have daily contact, and while I was still conscious of what he was doing, the contact was a lot less regular than it should have been. But it's like a friend who you don't see for a long time, then when you do you just pick up the conversation where it left off.

As a barrister you're on your own. So you've got to have that appetite for exploring the unknown, together with a certain belief that you've built the skills to cope with it. When I was appointed Queen's Counsel in November 2015, Pat's was one of the first calls I received, and one of the first people whose call I returned. I really see that no matter where my career in the law goes, the genesis of it was with my early days with Pat. It permeates a lot of how I think about the law, and how I conduct myself.

There are an enormous number of people who have worked for and been mentored by Pat, and gone to the bar. He has affected so many people's careers because he takes an individual interest in each person.

My advice to others wanting a mentor is this—if you're interested in mentoring you need to seek it out and approach the person you want as a mentor. It doesn't have to be a formal arrangement, but put yourself in a position to soak up everything you can. You have to be very open to whatever they've got to share, whether it's what you expected or not, or whether you agree with it or not. Just be there to listen and learn and take from it the things that apply to you.

Reflections

For mentors

- How can you call out gender bias or discrimination when you see it occurring in your mentee's experience?
- How do you choose the mentoring style appropriate for the situation? In which circumstances would you choose to urge your mentee to take a particular career step versus allowing them to discover their own path?
- Where can you find opportunities to throw your mentee in at the deep end but provide safeguards to ensure she swims, not sinks?
- How can you encourage your mentee to trust her instincts?

For mentees

- Where can you find opportunities to 'play where the ball isn't' in your career?
- Which situations make you feel confident? How can you apply this confidence across other situations where you lack confidence?
- What are your self-confidence-busters? Which ones would you like to work on with your mentor?
- In the absence of a formal mentor program who can you seek out and approach as a possible mentor?
- What courageous steps or decisions have you made? In what ways have these decisions built up your courage?

Celebrating our difference

◇◇◇◇◇

Ruby Anandajayasekeram
& Keerthi Ravi

Senior Legal Counsel at Shell Australia &
Co-founder of Diverse Women's
Mentoring Association

Ruby Anandajayasekeram

Ruby Anandajayasekeram is a Senior Legal Counsel at Shell Australia and works virtually from Melbourne with culturally diverse teams from around the world supporting Shell's global downstream acquisitions, divestments and post-closing team in the Asia Pacific region. She has been with Shell since 2004 and has worked in both their Melbourne and London offices supporting a variety of Shell's businesses. Prior to that, she worked at Allens Arthur Robinson (now Allens Linklaters). Ruby is passionate about and actively champions diversity and inclusion initiatives both within her organisation and externally, with a particular focus on the legal profession. She has had many successful mentoring relationships over her career, both as a mentor and as a mentee.

Keerthi Ravi

Keerthi has recently completed a Judge's Associateship in the Supreme Court and has recently co-founded the Diverse Women's Mentoring Association, a non-profit association which matches diverse women with mentors from professional services backgrounds, largely based on her experiences of being mentored by wonderful people such as Ruby.

Ruby's story

Education, sacrifice, family

From as early as I can remember, my parents instilled three core values in me—the power of education, the significance of sacrifice, and the importance of family. It is impossible to understand who I am without understanding my parents' story. Both Sri Lankan, they met and fell in love at university. Their love story and marriage challenged both the religion and the class distinction norms of the day. Despite their different backgrounds, they both recognised the power of education to provide opportunities in life and sought high educational success for all their children.

Sacrifice and family values are an integral part of their story. When my dad received a scholarship to study his PhD in Canada, my parents needed to choose whether to go their separate ways or marry and move overseas so my dad could pursue his doctorate. Recognising the long-term value of this opportunity for their future family, they left their country of origin as newlyweds with only 75cents to their name and a strong determination to build a better life for their children—a typical migrant story but also a decision which required my mum to sacrifice her own education and career. At this time, the civil war had started in Sri Lanka, so my family continued to follow my dad's career and the different countries it took him before we migrated to Australia.

How I see myself and how others see me

I am often asked the question 'Where are you from?' I respond by saying I'm Australian, which then triggers the next question 'Yes, but where are you *really* from?' How do I answer that question when although my parents are Sri Lankan, the first time I visited the island was only two years ago? Let alone that I was born in Canada, grew up in Kenya and Tanzania where I went to international schools, had short stints in Mexico and Jamaica, all before coming to Australia at the age of thirteen.

These conversations have made me realise that there are two realities in life—your own image of yourself, and then how others see you. Navigating your career, and life more broadly is about understanding and reconciling these two realities. Mentoring affords an opportunity to both mentors and mentees to facilitate this understanding and reconciliation.

Others will often judge you first by the way you look and, if you look different to them, will assume you come from a different cultural heritage and possess different values. Yet whilst appearing different to many around me, I don't define myself by this outward difference. Instead, whilst celebrating my cultural heritage, I define myself as Australian and believe that hard work and merit have been the basis of my achievements, and that I have been judged on those factors alone rather than on the colour of my skin or my cultural heritage.

That is not to say I have been immune from biases and assumptions in my career, but from my perspective, these probably stemmed from my gender rather than my cultural heritage. After having my daughter, people (with good intentions) sometimes assumed my commitment to family would be at the expense of my career, without necessarily asking me whether those assumptions were valid. In some ways, I similarly applied my own unconscious biases, values and assumptions when I became a mother. Having been brought up with a mother at home and a father who worked, I naturally assumed it was my role to be the primary carer. But I also wanted to have it all—seamlessly balance motherhood with a successful, uninterrupted career. When I tried to return to full time work, I really struggled and this dream hit a reality check. My wonderful husband stepped in and offered to work part-time to care for our daughter, and when we discussed it, it never occurred to me that we could have had that conversation earlier—I had simply assumed it was my job to care for our child and juggle my career while he continued to work full-time. Everyone has a different journey and needs to work out what works best for them as a family. Once he stepped in, I have really understood the value of letting go, to ask for support and not attempt to control everything.

Balancing motherhood and my career has brought to the foreground the importance of challenging traditional assumptions and biases in order to reconcile how I see myself and how others see me.

Encouraging this thought process in a mentee is an essential aspect of being a mentor.

'I felt honoured and privileged when Keerthi contacted me.'

I have experienced the power of mentoring as a mentee myself. I have been lucky to be mentored by some amazing people throughout my career and I attribute a large part of my success to mentors believing in me, encouraging me to move outside of my comfort zone, and actively sponsoring me. My first mentoring experience was provided through a professional association, and recently I looked back on the application form and was surprised to see that I had asked for a female mentor. I can't recall why I made this request but I suspect I was looking for a role model in the days when senior women were in the minority in the legal profession, and perhaps I thought I would feel more comfortable and safer opening up to someone who I thought would be more like me and would have faced similar challenges. As it turned out, I was matched to a male mentor who was amazing, who challenged my thinking and pushed me to think laterally and out of the box in a way that I may not have experienced otherwise. One of the most valuable pieces of advice I remember receiving from him was 'Don't wait until someone recognises you. Put your hand up. Tell people and be heard.'

This advice resonated with me in the context of my cultural upbringing. Early in my career, I had been receiving feedback from my peers and manager that I possessed excellent judgment and was really good at my work, but lacked confidence in meetings. I was mystified by this feedback. I would never have described myself as lacking in confidence, so what was going on? Working through this feedback was a pivotal moment because I realised it was my cultural values at play. Having been brought up to respect my elders and not argue back, no one ever told me that when you go into meeting with senior people that set of values is not relevant. What I viewed as showing respect, others viewed as lack of assertiveness.

As my own career flourished I began to realise that a small

investment of my own time can make an enormous difference to the careers of others. I am energised by mentoring others, actively sponsoring them and opening up my networks—and it's a two way street—I continue to learn so much from my mentees.

My neighbour, Randell, asked me one day about how people approach me to be their mentor. 'Well, they just ask—simple as that, or it happens organically' I replied. 'Really—that's all there is to it? Then I'm going to introduce you to this amazing woman. I think you would connect really well and I think she could benefit from just meeting you.'

I then met Keerthi, this amazingly talented woman who had already accomplished so much so early in her career. Keerthi and I had an initial natural and comfortable connection because of our cultural heritage and common understanding of cultural value systems which helped to establish trust quickly.

> *There were a lot of things that Keerthi did not have to explain to me because I 'understood'. But it was our diversity of experiences and perspectives that brought the most value to our relationship.*

Early on, I knew that Keerthi could achieve whatever she wanted. Yet Keerthi described herself in quite narrow ways. I encouraged her to think outside the box, to think more broadly and to consider other options. This is a key role for mentors—to challenge your mentee's thinking and stimulate them to think differently, to help them see things that they might not see because of their own blind spots, and to help them maximise their potential.

I also recognised the importance of connecting Keerthi to some of my network. 'Interested in in-house roles? Then let me connect you with …', 'Considering working overseas? Then you must talk to …'. Asking is an incredibly powerful thing that women in particular don't do enough of. People are always prepared to share their experiences or provide advice. Just asking someone for a chat can lead to so many different opportunities. I saw my role as facilitating the connection, and then Keerthi could make of it as she wanted.

The special role of mentors

I believe in having a diverse range of many mentors throughout your life. I see them like a board of advisors, with each bringing a different perspective and lens to situations at different times in your life.

I believe mentors have a number of special roles to play in helping to shape their mentee's career. First, mentors give their mentees confidence—they are able to see your potential when you might not see it and they can instil confidence in mentees to feel comfortable about speaking up about their own achievements. Mentors validate that it's okay to talk about your accomplishments without sounding like you are blowing your own trumpet. Secondly, mentors are not just there to build confidence they can also help to build visibility. The relationship may also naturally evolve into sponsorship, which is what happened between Keerthi and I. Sponsorship is powerful. Mentors can build their mentee's visibility through introductions—just one sentence in an email to a network will resonate and they will take it further.

Tapping into the diversity of experience in any relationship helps each one of us realise our human potential. Yet often as migrants we just want to integrate and be like everyone else. As kids we want the ham and cheese sandwich for school lunch, not the rice and curry mum packs in our school lunchbox. Funny though, how all the kids at school wanted to swap their ham and cheese sandwiches for lunches—they appreciated our difference more than we did, as kids perhaps we should have celebrated ours more.

Shell has provided me with a great career where I continue to learn and be challenged. I've worked in London as well as Melbourne and in my most recent role, Shell has been incredibly supportive in enabling me to work virtually, as the only lawyer based in Melbourne (my hometown) supporting matters in the Asia Pacific region. I also lead a global community of Shell lawyers, designed to capture, share and leverage our legal knowledge and experience in the areas of health, safety, security, environment and social performance. It's been a great role where I have had the opportunity to work with culturally diverse teams from all around the world, and continues to be a great adventure for me.

Shell uses the iceberg of differences diagram to explain the dynamics of diversity and I think this is a really useful metaphor. There are the characteristics you possess that are above the water line—the obvious things people see about you, to do with your gender, age and cultural background. Then there are the characteristics that are more hidden, or below the waterline. These may include your life experience, values, perspectives, thought processes, education, family background, motivators, or status in the community—all the other factors that together make up who you are as a person. Diversity and inclusiveness (and in my view, successful mentoring) is about recognising, understanding and including the whole person, not just what is obvious and can be seen. Once those underlying characteristics are activated, we can bring our whole selves to a relationship and realise our full potential. We are all different, we all have different experiences and we can all learn from each other. Having many mentors from diverse backgrounds is not only beneficial for individuals, but also the workplace and the broader community.

I was honoured and privileged that Keerthi reached out to me—I have loved being her mentor and I have learned so much from her.

Keerthi's story

I was born in India but became a 'citizen of the world' almost immediately. My family followed my father's career and the places to which it took us included Oman, Kuala Lumpur and eventually Australia. Fitting in to different cultures and environments was not a problem for me from an early age—attending international schools meant I developed friendships with children from diverse backgrounds as a natural way of growing up.

I grew up with a very strong and consistent message from my parents and grandparents—that you must be educated, and that you have a responsibility to your family and generations to come to do something worthwhile with that education. My parents sacrificed their own careers by moving to Australia so that we, their children, could have a better life. This sacrifice came with an implied responsibility, that the good education I was given be used to carve out a better life for myself and generations to come, and that studying hard and building a successful career was the path to such prosperity.

The power of one

My parents often remind me of my passion to lead as a young child—being the class prefect at school, being in charge and bossing my friends around, and telling everyone what to do. Then, for the first time, when I arrived in Australia I had difficulty assimilating at school and for a while I totally lost my confidence. I was first enrolled in a school where I was the only non-Anglo Saxon student in a school full of Anglo Saxon boys and girls where my differences—e.g. my accent (which was hard to pinpoint given the diversity of education I had already received), cultural habits (bringing Indian food to school was quite peculiar) and desire to be competitive in the classroom (I found it bizarre that there were no exams at primary school level)—I believe, damaged by self confidence. I subsequently moved to Cheltenham Primary School (a credit to my father who saw how miserable I was) and went on to Macrobertson Girls High School, both schools where there were many students from diverse cultural backgrounds, and suddenly I wasn't the only different girl anymore, and I flourished again. I recall one teacher at Cheltenham Primary in particular, who took an interest in me, recognised my potential and instilled in me the confidence to overcome my apprehensions and insecurities. Almost overnight I totally changed, reverting back to my natural leadership talents and within six months I became school captain. Restoring my confidence in this way was an incredible legacy left by that one teacher.

'You must meet Ruby. She's done it all.'

I always wanted to be a lawyer from a very young age and I followed that dream. After graduating my law degree I began working at Corrs, a large commercial law firm. It was here where I confided to Randell, a work colleague, friend and mentor, about my aspiration to facilitate mentoring opportunities for women with diverse cultural backgrounds. The initiative, the Diverse Women's Mentoring Association (DWMA), was launched in 2017 but back then it was still a dream. At the same time, I had just been offered the role of a Judge's Associate and was contemplating whether this would be the best next career move for me. After confiding in Randell about these dilemmas he told me: 'You must meet this neighbour of mine, called Ruby. She has a very similar cultural background and upbringing to you.' He had been talking about Ruby all year, and would speak very highly of her: 'She's done it all, is a bit older than you and has a very successful career. She might be a good person for you to get to know' he said.

It was as simple as connecting with Ruby on LinkedIn and the relationship immediately blossomed. The hallmark of our relationship is minimal rules; other than agreeing to confidentiality, meeting regularly and me coming prepared, the relationship has been shaped by my particular circumstances and needs at the time.

I have had the benefit of many professional mentors throughout my career and I credit much of my success to their influence.

However there is something special about the relationship with Ruby. We have only known each other for six months, but having a similar background, family experiences and values allowed us to communicate in a deeper way and I felt safe in sharing my more personal family journey with Ruby for the first time.

What do we discuss in our mentoring conversations? On a professional level, initially when I was at a career crossroads, I was looking for advice from a woman who had gone on that path before me. Looking back to those early days I recall being very targeted and funnelled in my vision—either stay in a law firm or go to the bar.

> *Ruby helped me broaden my horizons to consider possibilities I had not thought about. She opened up prospects, challenged my self-doubts and provided me with an assurance that I could explore new paths I otherwise wouldn't have had the courage to pursue.*

Ruby facilitated an initial connection with Allens Linklaters (of which she is an alumnus) which, in my view, played an integral part in securing my next role with Allens Linklaters, which I will commence in 2018.

These days our conversations range from how to address the challenges of being a culturally diverse female to family and personal challenges. The law profession seems to be coming to terms with gender diversity but still has a long way to go in accepting cultural diversity, in my view.

Ruby taught me to listen to my instincts and back my own judgment. These days if I am only eighty percent sure about a decision I am much more likely to proceed, whereas previously I would have to feel one-hundred percent sure. I am definitely less risk averse these days.

Just as importantly Ruby opened up her networks to enable me to speak with others in the legal and corporate worlds. I feel honoured that she had that level of faith in me. It's unlikely the relationship will come to an end; it's more likely to continue on a more informal basis. These days I just pick up the phone to Ruby—the days of formally requesting meetings, carefully crafting emails and double-checking her availability were important at the start, but are now behind me. I am about to move to Sydney and start a new phase in my career, so I will have a lot of questions to explore with Ruby.

On the home front, conversations these days are being dominated by my parents' desire for me to start a family—and I admit, I'm resisting being told what to do. I hear them say 'time to look for a husband, the body clock is ticking, time's running out, we will always be there to babysit'—not that they want me to give up my hard-won career for motherhood, far from it. They have an expectation that I have multi-tasked all my life and it's time to throw this into the mix. It gets back to sacrifice. Mum reminds her she had to give up things for her family and it's the same with me—'don't be too selfish,' she urges, 'think about what's right for everyone at a point in time.' Despite my resistance I realise her advice is a good reality check—I do want to be a mother at some stage, but at twenty-seven years of age, I reckon I have still got time to focus on my career for a while longer.

Sometimes I wonder if culturally diverse women have an added complexity to this parenthood challenge. If their cultural heritage demands women take on the total caring role and stigmatise men who would welcome taking on a caring role, the challenge to be both a professional woman and a mother can be enormous. My advice to women is make sure the person you marry values you as an equal and is willing to make their own sacrifices at certain stages—there's that word again: sacrifice.

I've learned so much

I used to believe that it was important to have a mentor from the same workplace who knows the workplace dynamics, now I am not so sure. Having a mentor removed from your workplace can be hugely beneficial. Ruby has no affiliation with the law firms or workplaces I have worked in and that strengthens the transparency of the relationship. Ruby can provide an honest, objective perspective and, as she does not know any of my bosses I can say anything to her without being concerned about breaching boundaries or that it will come back to haunt me.

My mentoring experience with Ruby also helped shape a better mentoring program through the DWMA. Being able to reflect on my own experiences, I can ask more targeted questions of mentors and mentees and structure the formal program in a more meaningful way. Ruby has also helped grow the association through opening up her networks who have subsequently offered to mentor young diverse women aspiring to become lawyers.

Reflections

Advice to mentors from Ruby

A few reflections I would share with other mentors or anyone considering becoming a mentor:

1. Make a difference—mentoring someone involves a very small investment of your time: for you as a mentor, it will be an enriching and rewarding learning experience, for your mentee, the mentoring opportunity could change their life.
2. Mentor many and mentor people who are different from you. The more different someone is to you, the more effort it may take to engage with them—but stick with it, it's worth it! When you mentor someone different from you, you will see the world from their perspective and they will see the world from yours—what you both learn from those experiences will help you to embrace diversity, feel more comfortable with difference, and more importantly will make you a more inclusive person. These experiences will also help to create the next generation of inclusive leaders.
3. Don't underestimate the power of your networks and be generous in creating connection opportunities for your mentee. If you feel comfortable promoting your mentee, sponsor them—it can make a huge difference to their career.
4. Successful mentoring relationships can't be forced. In my experience, the most successful relationships evolve organically and both parties must be authentic, committed to, and invested in nurturing the relationship.

Advice to new mentees from Keerthi

When reflecting on my own journey, there are two key insights around mentoring that I think are particularly relevant to culturally diverse women:

1. Don't focus on cultural diversity. This may sound counter-intuitive, but don't approach the relationship from a cultural similarity perspective, which can put an unhelpful lens on conversations. Instead, approach it with a fresh pair of eyes, as you would any new mentoring relationship. Being different is a strength and it's good to celebrate difference but don't let it define the relationship.
2. Avoid the echo chamber. When I started on my journey I believed I needed to connect with as many lawyers as possible. Eventually I learned not to fixate on selecting a mentor from a particular cultural background or professional or personal experience. If you want to be a successful lawyer, for example, it doesn't necessarily mean lawyers must mentor you. Whilst there is comfort in common language and experiences, you risk only hearing what your peers think, and reinforcing your own worldview. Hearing the perspectives of someone from a different background can be very powerful. It may help open up opportunities you had never dreamed of, or have conversations about career directions that you may never have with someone in your own professions. The world is a small place and there is no such thing as a bad mentor or bad connection. There are only a few degrees of separation from you and the rest of the world.

Whilst similar cultural heritage and shared values facilitated an initial connection between Keerthi and Ruby, ultimately the strength, substance and value of their relationship thrived from the diversity of their experiences and the different perspectives that they brought to the table.

Behind every great scientist is a great mentor

◇◇◇◇◇

Lynn Corcoran & Delphine Merino
Walter and Eliza Hall Institute

Lynn Corcoran

Lynn is a professor at the Walter and Eliza Hall Institute of Medical Research in Melbourne. In 2009, along with Director Doug Hilton and Professor Terry Speed, Lynn established the Institute's Gender Committee to help female staff members with family and career transitions.

Delphine Merino

Delphine has been mentored on and off by Lynn for two years. She completed her PhD in France before arriving in Australia to work for almost ten years as a post-doctoral fellow ('postdoc') at the Walter and Eliza Hall Institute of Medical Research. She is currently a mentor herself for several PhD students and post-docs, and is now leading her own group of researchers at the Olivia Newton John Cancer Research Institute.

Lynn's story

Mentoring programs

Our formal mentoring program was originally established to stop the leakage of good postdocs from the Institute, especially women. The post-doctoral stage is a critical transitional one in their career, they either move up or move out. We want to retain them so we created a formal mentoring program for this group. The formal program was not that successful but the relationships that developed were good, so the program ended up morphing to a more informal arrangement. The informal system seems to work more smoothly. We just get together when one of us feels that it's an important time or something's happened that we'd like to discuss.

I offered myself as a mentor through this program, and Delphine contacted me. For the last six years I was the Chairman of the Gender Equity Committee. I've been involved a lot in women's issues here, and doing things to help women along during family and career transitions, so Delphine would have known me from these activities and identified me as someone who could support and guide her.

Delphine was a senior postdoctoral fellow and has had a very successful career in a really competitive area. Working in this environment has been a very important learning experience for her, and her supervisors supported her during her career, but she felt it was time to look to the next stage in her career. She was at a critical juncture, transitioning to a state of independence. She wanted to start her own laboratory, which would entail moving up and sideways into a different institute or department. To do this she needed to attract grant money for independent research unrelated to her current laboratory and I provided feedback on her grant applications. With a low national success rate of about fifteen percent or less for grant applications, everyone could use some support.

I've been on assessment panels and peer review panels so I've assessed quite a few grant applications and now recognise what panels need to be convinced about the merits of an application. In some sections of Delphine's applications, she could have been a bit more strategic and self-promoting. I could empathize with her—I used to write in a semi-apologetic way myself in the early days of grant applications—and it wasn't until I began to look at the way male applicants put themselves forward, and how they presented themselves in a much more positive and assertive way, that I realised I needed to be much more self-confident and self-promoting.

Personality and values

Delphine and I have got different personalities. I'm an extroverted North American. I've been here for forty years, but I still have that American brashness. I hold strong opinions and I'm not afraid to express them. Delphine is a strong, though soft-spoken French woman who doesn't like conflict, despite her desire to push boundaries. Some of that makes her a great team member. But some of that also means she needed guidance to move forward as fast as she deserves to. She's a very talented person and she's comfortable reaching out to other senior people if she sees an area of overlap or a potential connection in her research.

Despite our differences we feel the same sympathies and have the same values. We are both female scientists who have been parents and we understand the problems of underselling yourself, and of compromise and not feeling as successful as others. We've both experienced times when we've been unsuccessful and it's really hurt our ego and self-confidence. I'm older than she is, so I went through the same stage maybe fifteen or twenty years before her. I see a lot of young women who are having children but also trying to gain some professional autonomy. They are going through the same things I have gone through. We actually have more in common than we have differences.

Strategic guidance

Mentoring in this context is similar to strategic guidance, because we operate in a very rigid structure of the grant cycle. Nobody here has a tenured position—everybody is on grant money that lasts for three to five years. We apply for grants mostly to a single body, and there are things you need to be able to do to make yourself attractive according to their criteria. I was not going to tell Delphine how to do science because we worked in different areas. But I could give her advice about how to get involved in the peer review process, or what community work to do; to think of ways of satisfying all of those expectations.

> *I learnt early on that mentors should never interfere on behalf of the mentee.*

I'm not too shy about approaching people within the Institute because I've been here since the 1980s, and many here were friends of mine as students, even the director. I wouldn't be uncomfortable asking him, without naming names, what he thought of a situation. But I would never intervene on Delphine's behalf without her okay. She understood that while I might have strong opinions, I would never do anything that might get her into trouble.

On gender

There was a time in the early or mid-nineties when most female laboratory heads at our institute had to make life-changing decisions to pursue their careers in science. Most either married a scientist, or never married, or never had children. But I've learned that women of Delphine's generation are amazingly capable and remarkably connected; they think much more ambitiously than in my time. They're deserving of the success they have won. They seem braver to me. It's fantastic. I can't imagine myself being as independent a thinker as early as that.

Lots of women say they like to have *women* mentors. I get that, because how does a woman navigate these waters? But I also think it's great to have a man as a mentor, because a man doesn't think about limitations. We can learn from men who would just say, 'For heaven's sake, don't worry about it, just do it!' rather than have the self-limiting beliefs that hold back some women.

I haven't had one person in my career who I would describe as a mentor. I've had two or three during my working life who have been friends and bosses at the same time. Some men have put me forward and encouraged me to apply for roles that I might not otherwise have applied for. They were great referees for me. I had a female friend who worked here, who was about ten years older than me. She's now retired. She never reached as high a status as she might have if she was a guy. But she was kind of a no-nonsense person, with good judgment—very wise. She was one of those women who at that time didn't feel they could have children because it would impede their progress, so she's very interested in my daughter and we have a close family relationship. But she would advise me on strategic issues also.

What would you like mentoring to be?

Two aspects are important in mentoring. First, the mentee should drive the relationship. Otherwise, if the mentor has to organise the next meetings he or she ends up acting like a boss and then the mentee thinks 'Heck, I have to prepare something for this meeting.' It becomes a duty then. I think making it regular and relaxed helps a lot. Secondly mentors need to be taught how to be mentors. Otherwise mentors probably just talk about what they did, and that may not be the best way to support the mentee.

One thing I would change about my relationship with Delphine is to meet more often, not necessarily just when there's an issue—just meet to keep tabs on one another, and get to know one another. There's nothing to talk about? We talk about our kids. If it's something else, we talk about that. My other suggestion to mentees is to have a couple of mentors who present different points of view, and who should probably talk to each other about what each one of them is trying to help the mentee with.

Mentoring relationships may come to a logical conclusion, or ebb and flow over time. For instance, the relationship could be more acute during the transition period from dependence to independence, like Delphine's situation. Once the mentee is established in her own independent stream, the relationship could be less intense. By that stage a mentee would be well known in the Institute and could probably progress further by talking to her peers, rather than with somebody more senior. But I think there's always a possibility that there could be some ongoing advice and support.

Delphine's story

Choosing a mentor

When a new mentoring program was offered at the Walter and Eliza Hall Institute of Medical research, I was entering a challenging, but exciting transition period, where I decided to move into an independent position. I chose Lynn, for a number of reasons.

Firstly, we share similar values. Lynn is respected in our institute for her assertiveness, honesty and commitment, and I felt she was someone I could trust, someone that would encourage me with great enthusiasm. While I am, by far, less extroverted than Lynn, I am quite assertive. Lynn has also helped me to bring this out in my writing. We share similar beliefs, and are both women with similar parenting situations; I knew I could learn a lot from her.

Secondly it was important to have someone who was relatively senior, with a good understanding of the system. Indeed, Lynn faced the difficulties and the politics of our system a long time before me, and was strategically positioned to provide guidance. She was chair for the Gender Equity in Science Committee, and well connected in the Australian scientific community.

Lastly Lynn was not directly involved in my projects, and I thought she would have a good objective point of view on my situation. She was able to provide constructive feedback on my performance and advice on important decisions.

It's not about science, it's about strategy

The first time I interacted with Lynn was well before the mentoring program. She was part of a 'simulated panel', composed of several senior people from our institute, to help me prepare for an important fellowship interview. The mentoring therefore began long before its 'official' start date. And I hope it will continue despite my move to a new institute, and to a more senior position.

Lynn provides great advice on funding, and career strategy. When I met Lynn I knew what my objectives were. We discussed what funding strategies I needed to pursue, as she knew enough about my projects to tell me which grants to apply for and which to let go. Lynn also knew many senior leaders in our institute, and was able to advise me on various political issues while I was trying to find a 'host' laboratory. I was expecting her to alert me about any opportunities that she would hear about, networking and connections. A mentorship at our level is not about science, but more about strategy. Lynn helped me to navigate the politics in the workplace.

Lynn also helped me to promote myself in my CV and in a draft application for funding. One of the issues I sought her advice about was how to describe my maternity leave in these documents. Lynn provided particularly valuable feedback on this section. Initially, I justified that whilst on maternity leave I was unable to supervise students, attend conferences or continue with research, on an apologetic tone. Lynn helped me to reword my achievements in a dramatically more positive way: despite two career disruptions in the last five years, I made some major contributions in my field of research, published several publications, and obtained a fellowship. Furthermore, the English language has been a barrier for me, and this includes some cultural differences. When French people use the adjective 'good', Australian (or Americans like Lynn) use 'outstanding'; it is important to use the right words and promote ourselves according to the culture and environment in which we are living. Lynn helped me to reword some achievements along these lines.

Being a mentee

What I expect of a mentor is career guidance; this includes highlighting opportunities for career advancement and growth, taking me out of my comfort zone and giving me a fresh perspective on my situation. The mentoring experience reassured me that I was on the right track in a highly competitive system. We live in a world of perfectionism, and this is particularly true in the scientific industry. Therefore, it is really important to receive objective performance feedback. Lynn guided me on where to focus and how to manage conflicts of interest.

> *It is especially important to have a high degree of trust in the relationship. Most of my discussions with Lynn were focussed on defining my career choice and holding tactful negotiations.*

I was meeting with different senior scientists at that time, and I knew that Lynn would not interfere with my actions and would be my 'advocate' if I asked.

I particularly enjoyed Lynn's positive attitude and enthusiasm about her work. I remember from our first discussion with Lynn she reminded me to choose a fun work environment. This is such a positive piece of advice and I can see that Lynn has lived this advice in the way she works too.

Becoming a mentor

When I first became a mentor we held a speed-dating session with forty PhD students and ninety post-docs where we only had two minutes to tell the students about ourselves. I was chosen by my mentee because she was in the same lab where I did my first post-doc, so there was some common ground. I expect her to contact me according to her needs. I will also be proactive in looking out for any opportunities she may want to pursue, just like Lynn has done for me.

At this stage of my career I find mentoring especially stimulating. At the same time, I receive advice from my peers, who naturally 'empathise' with my situation (in an encouraging way), and younger researchers who can easily connect with me and come to me for advice. Mentoring is very gratifying. It is a special relationship that can sometimes be difficult to maintain in our busy lives, if it wasn't part of an implicit and 'contractual' agreement. In my opinion an informal program can sometimes work more effectively and flexibly than a formal arrangement. It is also about helping each other through challenging situations. It is wonderful to know you've got someone looking out for you.

Male versus female mentoring

When I entered the program as a mentee, it so happened that I chose someone who had succeeded as a woman and a parent. I would like to address each of these aspects separately: being a woman, and being a parent.

I initially didn't want to choose my mentor according to gender, but the fact that my mentor was a woman was a bonus. There are very few women who reach the top leadership role in science, and they all have their different ways of succeeding. Lynn has been a strong advocate for women's rights throughout her career, and has good insights into these issues. Having said that, I was extremely fortunate to be also mentored by men from my institute and other institutes, including the director of WEHI, Professor Doug Hilton, known as a 'male champion of change'. The advice, encouragement and guidance of these men were infinitely valuable at crucial transition times. We never defined these relationships as mentor/mentee relationships, but they were.

I believe that 'behind every great scientist, there are great mentors', independent of their gender. Throughout my career I encountered several men in similar situations to me and I know they also needed support and mentoring regardless of their gender. The challenge of juggling competing demands of parenting and progressing our careers is experienced by both genders.

During my first discussion with Lynn, we found out that both of us have a daughter. I remember that she encouraged me to consider having a second child. I knew—from her knowledge on gender equity issues—that by saying that, she was encouraging me to build my family at the same time as progressing my career. It made me smile at the time, as I was actually in the early stage of my second pregnancy, and found it extremely encouraging that someone would give me this up-front advice in a professional environment.

Later, Lynn gave me valuable advice on how to describe my career trajectory in funding applications. I have two children and I took only three months of maternity leave each time. This practice is well accepted in France, but not so much in Australia where I experienced a cultural clash. Despite this, I felt comfortable with my decision, and received support from the institute to manage these career disruptions in the best way I could, through childcare support and technical assistance during my leave. This support made a huge difference for women in science, and Lynn has been part of this vital movement.

I believe mentoring is essential at every stage of our careers. I am mentoring both men and women starting their careers, and I have developed many important relationships with several mentors. I will always value the relationship that I have with Lynn. In addition, having a mentor who can role model good mentoring is a wonderful way to become a good mentor and a good manager yourself.

The best piece of advice from my mentor

In a male dominated and highly competitive workplace, I have been told early on that I was not 'aggressive enough' to succeed. And yet, I have the motivation and desire to lead the big 'career battle' in a non-aggressive but determined way. In this context, the best advice I received was 'Show them your style'. Lynn never tried to change me, never implied I should be following a certain style to succeed; she encouraged me to be true to myself and confident in my own values. I remember receiving similar advice about parenting; there is not one single way to be a good parent; combine your own set of skills, follow your own rules, and be consistent. This is a fabulous way to embrace diversity in our society and work-places.

Reflections

For mentors:

- What specifically can you bring to the mentoring relationship? What attributes can you best offer your mentee?
- What does your mentee want from the relationship?
- How can you support your mentee identify what she believes in and stands for?
- What are the similarities and differences in values and style between you and your mentee? How can you have a conversation with your mentee about these differences? How can you leverage these differences to encourage your mentee to broaden her perspective and see the world differently?
- What can you specifically do to create a climate of confidentiality and mutual trust? What could break that trust?
- What practical steps can you take to ensure you meet regularly, are dealing with issues that matter and the relationship thrives, without taking away the responsibility of the mentee to drive the process?

For mentees:

- What do you want of the relationship at this stage of your career? Do you want someone to push you, or support and encourage you? Are you seeking practical advice or a sounding board? Are you looking for a role model? Are you seeking access to your mentor's networks?
- How can you get to know your mentor at the outset to decide if she is right for you?
- What are the characteristics you need in a mentor to feel supported but also challenged at the right times?
- Is a female mentor right for you, or should you seek a male mentor? Why?

- What can you learn from a mentor with a different personality and approach to you?
- What is one capability that will make the biggest difference to your career success at this point? How strong are you in this capability? How can you develop this capability?

Pushing the boundaries

◇◇◇◇◇

Adam Fennessy & Kate Houghton

formerly at Victorian Department of Environment, Land, Water & Planning

Adam Fennessy PSM

Adam was the Secretary of the Victorian Department of Environment, Land, Water and Planning (DELWP) from January 2015 to June 2017 and a Victorian Male Champion of Change. His vision for DELWP was for a diverse, inclusive and gender equitable workforce that reflects the communities it serves. Flexible working arrangements and innovative thinking were key planks underpinning this vision. Adam encouraged his senior executive team to coach and mentor others in the department, creating fulfilling careers and a workplace that attracts, retains and develops the best. Adam is now a partner in the professional services firm EY.

Kate Houghton

Kate is Deputy Secretary of Water and Catchments. Kate and Adam's professional working relationship dates back to when they were colleagues in the Victorian Department of Premier and Cabinet (DPC) in the early 2000s. Although their careers diverged, they have kept in touch through some critical times. Their career paths crossed again when Adam appointed Kate to his senior executive team at the Department of Environment and Primary Industries, DELWP's predecessor department, in 2013. Kate is now Deputy Secretary, Crime Prevention.

Adam's story

The ties that bind—capability and shared values

Kate and I first worked together at DPC. We hadn't met before, but we worked out quickly that we had similar values: integrity, honesty and transparency. When you have a shared understanding of what is important, it makes work conversations easier. Our professional relationship grew from there.

Kate later came to work for me during the restructure of the Department of Environment and Primary Industries (DEPI), out of which came the new DELWP. She had proactively kept in touch with me so I knew she was ready to return to work after taking parental leave, and would be willing to try something new. On her first day, I could sense she felt like an outsider and was coming in with no networks—however, I knew her reputation and contacts were still strong. I also learned from Kate that her next role would need to be flexible, so I offered her a new role on a fully flexible basis to set up a new policy team within my departmental division. She then established the team and recruited some incredibly talented people in the process.

Where are the women?

When the Department of Sustainability and Environment merged with the Department of Primary Industries in 2013, and I was appointed Secretary, there was a lack of women in our executive team. I knew if we strove for a more consciously diverse approach, we would attract some great talent. I asked Kate and another senior executive to prepare a gender equity action plan. The plan recommended a target of forty percent women and I remember asking, 'Why not go for fifty percent?' I was a bit stunned by some of the reactions we received when we announced this. One man said to me, 'This isn't going to work out well in the long term for us.' He meant 'us men', suggesting there would be fewer opportunities for men.

I recognised that I could attract some great people to work for me if I offered flexible working arrangements. As I had come to the department on flexible working arrangements myself, I was able to demonstrate that I genuinely supported it. I also started encouraging senior leaders across the department to adopt a coaching and mentoring approach in the way they lead. Around this time, I was also appointed a Male Champion of Change, which reinforced my belief in the powers of diversity and inclusion to drive culture and performance.

The role of a mentor

Kate and I never discussed establishing a mentoring relationship. She never asked me, 'Can you be my mentor?' and I never made a conscious decision that I would take her on as a mentee. I don't think of myself as Kate's mentor—more of a supporter and advocate because she's already really good at what she does.

A large part of mentoring is giving someone encouragement, confirmation and confidence. There are concrete experiences I can give Kate and then there's symbolic signaling, which is just as important. Appointments should be based on an individual's capabilities to do the job, and not solely a product of relationships.

I initially supported and advocated for Kate because I wanted our organisation to benefit from her talent, capability and clear potential as a senior executive leader. I also began to see that gender diversity and flexibility is not just good for our organisation, but critical for our broader success with the community. It's important that we reflect our community by having diverse and gender balanced executive teams, which is essential to make sure we make the best decisions and achieve the best outcomes for our community.

Kate once said she didn't want to become the 'poster girl' for flexible working, and to feel that she had to make it work for every other woman in this department. Having my own family, and sharing the load with my wife when she was working, I empathised with her need for flexibility. Because I've had that experience of seeking to balance family and work, I respect Kate's time away from the office. If it's a Friday afternoon and I know Kate's at her daughter's netball training, I won't call her unless I absolutely need to (and even then, nothing is usually that urgent that it can't wait).

My advice to mentors is simply to listen. I'm an extrovert, so I have to keep reminding myself to stop talking and start listening. Also, be open to learning from your mentees. I'm involved in a few informal mentor/mentee relationships, and the best ones are where I learn as much from my mentees as they do from me.

Resisting the echo chamber

Although having similar values is important, there are times when it's good to hear from people with a totally different set of values and experiences. Otherwise I could drift into a comfortable space where I'd only listen to people who reflect my own values and reinforce my own beliefs.

> *Sometimes you need other people to challenge you to get out of that 'echo chamber'. That is also part of the role of being a mentor too I think.*

Someone who has been a real mentor for me is Cheryl Batagol. While we don't have a formal arrangement, I'll seek Cheryl out if something interesting is happening and we'll have dinner or coffee a couple of times a year. We have a professional sort of relationship because she's the Chair of one of our government statutory authorities, the Victorian Environment Protection Agency. I recently went to a book launch for Women World Changers and was asked to nominate someone who had influenced me. I nominated Cheryl and that was my way of thanking her. I also have other figures who support and inspire me, including the Federal Sex Discrimination Commissioner, and convenor of our Male Champions of Change group, Kate Jenkins, from whom I've learned a lot, and openly adopted ideas from—especially around transforming culture.

Reverse mentoring

I've learnt a lot from my mentor relationship with Kate and one key lesson has been not to make assumptions on behalf of others. Kate has taught me that it's fine to give your opinion, but ultimately what works for the other person can be the best option. This means being patient and supporting people at their own pace.

Kate has also shown me that it's important to be open and clear about your family life as well as your working life. It takes a lot of pressure off when people understand your family circumstances. I've learnt from Kate not to try to perpetuate a myth that you can be an effective executive whose personal life is hidden away. Being a role model for flexibility and work life balance is so important for Kate and myself, and we both understand that people will look at what we do, not what we say. Ultimately Kate has shown me to listen to my intuition, and has helped me learn that good mentoring relationships work when you come away from them feeling energised.

Kate's story

My mentoring relationship with Adam has never been formal or structured. We unconsciously chose each other when we worked together at DPC. Our ethical framework and values are very similar, focusing on integrity, honesty and transparency. We both believe that the government sector should preserve public interest, defend public value and serve communities. These fundamentals formed the basis of a trusting relationship and gave us an authentic connection. We have kept in touch since then; from DPC, to Adam rising through the ranks of the Victorian Public Sector, to my two moves to Sydney and maternity leave. Every time I was leaving a job or Melbourne, I would get in touch with Adam to let him know what I was doing, not to ask for anything, but just to keep the connection strong.

This connection was especially important when I wanted to return to work after my second round of maternity leave. I was definitely not sitting at home thinking, 'They'll call and give me the job I want.' It was more along the lines of, 'Who is my strongest advocate and my supporter?' You can't do that unless you have fostered an ongoing relationship with people.

The conversation starters

The typical approach I take with Adam is to ask him lots of questions, like: 'Have you been in a similar situation? What was your instinct? How did it work out?' Or 'I'm a bit nervous about this. Am I thinking about this the right way? Are there gaps in my thinking?'

If Adam doesn't agree with one of my ideas, he won't say, 'Don't do it'—he is more likely to test my thinking. One time, I wanted to apply for an economic development role in DPC and Adam challenged me to think more deeply. He helped me reflect on what was driving my decisions, and whether I really wanted to go for that opportunity.

The confronting conversation

When my maternity leave ended, I considered going back to working as a specialist in the water sector. It was my background and my comfort zone, having worked in DPC, the EPA, and the Water and Catchments part of State Government. I called Adam for advice and discussed my thoughts with him. He challenged my thinking: 'Don't go with what's comfortable.' That was very difficult advice to take, because I needed stability and certainty. I needed to be able to do a job that I knew I could do, from A to Z and back again. But Adam said, 'You need to do something different. You've lost confidence in your capabilities. Think about jumping into something different, like environmental policy, in a small team which needs building.' I was not expecting him to say that. I called him just for advice, not for a specific role. The clincher came when Adam said, 'Look at your career aspirations. If you don't move now, when are you going to move?' That really got me thinking: if now is not the time, then I'm never going to jump. That was confronting.

Coming back from maternity leave was hard. I'm sure this is a common feeling; you know you're sort of good at being a mother, but you haven't practiced your professional craft for eighteen months. Going back to work in a new role, in a different environment, was challenging. I remember rocking up the first day and thinking, 'What am I doing? I don't know any of these people.' Adam had just completed a restructure and no-one knew me. I had no history with anyone, other than the boss. The advocacy and support from Adam was very important at that time, because I needed to build up my credibility from scratch. He'd put me on projects concerning government change, where I was negotiating with senior people in other departments. I had all this autonomy, and I really had to consolidate my skills.

Taking that role was one of the best things I ever did, because so much opened up for me. I think if I had just gone on with the same career, I would have got lost and buried. Pulling out of my comfort zone was really challenging, but the right thing to do.

The getting of wisdom

Adam is a great supporter of working with flexibility. The way he operates gives me confidence in the decisions I make with other women in the workplace. When I recruited a director from EPA, I wanted her diversity of thought as well as her diversity of gender. After I offered her the job, she told me she was pregnant. I still wanted her to take the job. When she asked, 'Did you hear what I said?' I replied, 'You can start in two months and then go on maternity leave. But I want you for your skills and leadership for the long term.' I'm not sure I would have had the confidence to make that call without Adam's leadership.

> *The greatest thing I've learnt from Adam is knowing that decision making is not always*

> *just about what's logical. I've learned to listen to my instincts, and that my feelings are good signposts to making decisions.*

For me, the right decision is about what's right for my family. When big decisions come up, Adam and I can have a conversation, but the decision actually gets made at home. I'm much more calm and confident about having a work-life balance. It still makes me nervous, but the more you do it, the better you get at it. I live by the creed that family comes first. If I begin prioritising work against family, then it's time to leave work. I know Adam shares these values around work-life balance too.

Adam is not my only mentor—I have other people I also call on for advice and I believe it's good to get different perspectives from other people who will challenge you. The chair of the EPA is an amazing person and leader with supersonic instincts. She will call me out of the blue and say, 'I think you need me.' And she'll be right. She will often tell me to just get over myself and stop being self-indulgent. Sometimes you need that shock every now and then, someone to tell you to get out of your own way.

My advice to mentees is to be as honest as you can in conversations with your mentor. The more you put into it, the more you'll get out of it. Secondly, don't expect them to tell you what you want to hear. Just let it happen, because you're going to get much more value out of it.

Reflections

For mentors:

- As an influential leader, how can you stimulate and champion a mentoring style across your leadership team?
- How can you encourage fresh bold thinking about flexibility in your organisation?
- What are the advantages and disadvantages of having different world views?
- How can you leverage this difference to constructively challenge your mentee's perspectives?
- Does your workplace adopt flexible work practices? How can you as a leader and mentor encourage the uptake of flexible work practices by all employees, not just women?
- What conversations could you have to encourage your mentee to bring her whole self to work?

For mentees:

- What are your values? Where did your values come from?
- How have your values influenced your career choices?
- How satisfied are you that you are living your values at work? If you are not totally satisfied what are three things you can do to better express your values in your work?
- How strong is your network? Who are your strongest advocates and supporters? How can you leverage these relationships at specific career turning points?
- What do you want in terms of flexible work practices? How can you convince your manager that your needs for flexibility will work for everyone?

Finding your voice

◇◇◇◇◇

Jodi Fullarton-Healey & Sophie Wilson

ANZ Bank & Salesforce

Jodi Fullarton-Healey

Jodi is General Counsel, Institutional Banking at ANZ Bank and leads a team of more than 100 lawyers located across Australia, Asia-Pacific, UK and USA. She arrived at ANZ Bank with a reputation as a top banking and finance specialist, with eighteen years' experience at the Australian law firm Blake Dawson (now Ashurst). Mentoring and coaching is integral to Jodi's leadership approach. She co-founded the Executive Committee of the Melbourne branch of Women in Banking & Finance (WIBF), which she chaired for two years; and was also a member of the WIBF National Executive Committee. It was at the inaugural WIBF Melbourne lunch where Jodi and Sophie met for the first time.

Sophie Wilson

Sophie is a Solution Engineer at Salesforce, a Fortune 500 company, which has the world's number one rated customer relationship management (CRM) software. She moved to Salesforce in 2016 after a stellar career with over seven years at ANZ , where she was recognised as one of the bank's top performers. Sophie attributes her relationship with Jodi as instrumental in giving her the self-confidence and courage to take a leap of faith into a totally new career in technology and innovation.

Jodi's story

I first met Sophie at a Women in Banking and Finance lunch. I watched this fascinating young woman ask interesting questions and take copious notes—she seemed a delightful person to get to know. 'Who is this bright spark sitting next to me?' I wondered. I decided I wanted to hang on to this one. So I asked her to give me a copy of her notes when she'd typed them up. That is how our relationship started. It was purely coincidence that we sat next to each other and our relationship blossomed from there.

Sophie started coming to my office every couple of months, and we'd catch up for a coffee and a chat. She never asked me to be her mentor, but a mentoring type relationship naturally developed over time. I love giving Sophie and other women like her the support, encouragement and advocacy that a mentoring relationship brings. It's something that I would have loved to have had when I was in the early stages of my career.

The big lessons for life

Our conversations range from quick catch-ups to exploring critical turning points in Sophie's life. My beliefs around building a successful career fall into six key messages, which Sophie and I regularly discuss and apply:

1. Make yourself indispensable to somebody
2. Build a broad experience base to ensure you are always in demand
3. Constantly seek feedback to guide your development
4. Lean in to discomfort. What is the worst that can happen?
5. Put yourself in the other person's shoes to truly understand their motivations; and
6. Remember you are playing the long game—all your experience should build towards achieving your long-term goals.

Like me, Sophie was ambitious and it was clear from the outset that she was impatient to get places fast. I remember coaching her to slow down, be patient, and get as much broad experience as she could. That way she'd be better prepared for all kinds of roles. I also encouraged her to do things a few times, not just once, to consolidate her learning and experience. No-one knows what the future holds, but if you have broad experience it can take you to so many places, whether it is the next secondment or a permanent move.

I encouraged Sophie to throw her hat in to the ring for several roles that she might not have otherwise considered, and if she didn't succeed to be willing to accept the consequences and listen to the reasons why she may have missed out. Understanding how others see you is critical, particularly how they perceive your skill set and areas for development. I knew she needed to be tenacious about inviting feedback because in my experience people are reluctant to provide it. So, I encouraged her to be specific, to ask probing questions like 'What am I not doing? What am I doing too much of? Why did you select that person over me?' Although listening to those answers can be uncomfortable, the feedback is also extremely important and Sophie could use this feedback to make better informed decisions about how she could develop her working style.

Leaning in to discomfort

I had many conversations with Sophie about getting out of her comfort zone. There are times when staying in your comfort zone is the right thing to do. For some women that time may come when they have young children, are totally sleep-deprived and just need to work on automatic pilot for a while. But they shouldn't stay there for too long, or soon they'll wonder why everyone else is moving up the ladder and they are being left behind. As her mentor, I was in a position to encourage Sophie to have a go. She was intelligent, capable and ambitious. If a role or a secondment didn't work out, she would be in high demand and something else would come up. I advised her to be noticed and be networked—that way she would always be in demand.

As part of these discussions I encouraged Sophie to apply for the Generalist Banker Program—a very challenging program designed for high potential future leaders. It would expose her to many different roles, and provide the opportunity for overseas postings. She was smart—a go-getter with enormous potential. This program was highly contested and only a few applicants would be selected, but I knew she could get into the program if she applied. Despite my best efforts, she wasn't inspired to apply. Ultimately it was her choice and other options came her way.

Strongest advocate and toughest critic

I was a great supporter of Sophie's in the bank. I shared my networks and advocated for her as often as I could. I helped prepare her for future roles and pushed her. She is capable of just about anything and has no qualms about openly promoting her capabilities. I think this has enabled her to become noticed. I encouraged her to act only after having all the facts, because that gives you confidence and credibility when you need to ask for something or express a point of view.

However, there are times when a mentor also needs to be the mentee's toughest critic, talking frankly and providing tough feedback when necessary. Not many people feel confident providing such feedback and if Sophie doesn't hear it from me, then from whom? I remember soon after Sophie had taken up the Salesforce role, she came to me feeling totally overwhelmed and exhausted, having to quickly come up to speed in a totally new industry sector, learn the technology at a breakneck pace and cope with an enormous workload. She asked me how she might create some semblance of work/life balance during this time. I could have empathised more with her, but I think I just said, 'Suck it up Sophie. It's not going to kill you. Remember the long game, and why you are doing this.' I felt she needed to hear the message that in the short-term pain is necessary for a longer-term gain.

You never truly know a person until you walk in their shoes

I am a great believer in looking at an issue from another person's perspective. When Sophie went to her boss with concerns about her workload, she was simply told her to organise her life better. I think that was a difficult message for Sophie to hear. But I thought that her boss may have interpreted Sophie's concern as a complaint. I encouraged Sophie to consider it from her boss's perspective and ask: 'How does this look to her? What do I need to know and understand about her?' Walking a mile in the shoes of the other person often takes the heat out of a conflict situation and develops a deeper relationship based on empathy and understanding.

Ingredients for a successful relationship

Sophie and I are bound by a similar set of values and that forms the foundation for the chemistry between us. We both recognise the importance of family in our lives. We both have a strong sense of justice. We are both perfectionists. We love working with people and collaborating with others, and we both have a great sense of humour (well, we think so!). It would be difficult to develop a sense of rapport if our values were vastly different. I do like to hear different perspectives from people with different values, but I'm not sure I would develop such a close bond with those people.

The greatest contribution a mentor can make to a mentee's life is to be selfless and generous with your time and support. Remember that the relationship is about them, not you. You are there for many reasons—to teach them to trust their intuition, to encourage them to have a go, to hold up a mirror and help them recognise their strengths and career needs. But in the end the right decision is the one that the mentee believes is best for them. It may not be one that the mentor might choose if they were in a similar situation, or one they hope the mentee will choose. It is the one that intuitively feels right for the mentee.

In my experience, a relationship that develops organically is stronger than one predetermined by a formal process. A formal process may be a good starting point, it can provide a framework for discussion and it sends strong messages internally about the importance of developing a mentoring culture. However, a relationship will only endure if it develops from a place of genuine respect. You will know you've got there when you simply enjoy each other's company. I look forward to our times together because we spend a lot of time laughing, not just solving major problems or dealing with crises.

Although mentoring is about being selfless, it does give mentors so much in return. It's fun having relationships with younger people like Sophie. I learn so much about their way of thinking.

It's also stimulating to have people in my life beyond my circle of friends. I get a great amount of satisfaction seeing Sophie grow and develop. She is so much more confident about saying what she feels now, and she is also a much better listener.

I encourage everyone to be on the lookout for the right mentor, then have the courage to start a mentoring relationship with them. It doesn't have to be based on a formal request like, 'Can you be my mentor?' It could simply be a suggestion to catch up for a coffee, then at the end ask: 'Do you mind if we do this again?' I believe people like helping others and will make time for you if they possibly can. If they genuinely don't have time, they may already be mentoring several people, so don't take it personally. Perhaps they can suggest another person for you to approach.

I would encourage women to cultivate relationships with male mentors too, and to not just seek out other women. Men still hold most of the positions of power, and we shouldn't underestimate the difficulty it takes to push women up the ladder. Besides, you get a different perspective from men than you would from other women. Take networking, for instance. Networking doesn't always come easily to women, whereas men do it naturally. It's just part of their life, something they do from early age. It is interesting to observe how men play sport—they may play rough on the field but then are best buddies after the game. Whereas women don't play team sports in the same way. We can hold grudges. Perhaps we have something to learn there.

Sophie's story

My lucky day when I met Jodi

'Oh my god, I've lucked in. I'm sitting next to this amazing woman.' Those were my first thoughts when I sat next to Jodi at the Women in Banking and Finance lunch. She was everything I aspired to be —impeccably presented, self-assured and confident. Jodi had a real presence. I knew I could learn a lot from her wisdom and experience. When she asked me for my notes at the lunch, I grabbed the opportunity to follow up with her. That was my lucky day, meeting Jodi.

We started catching up on a regular basis. Often I would call her, but she'd also follow up with me if she hadn't heard from me for a while. That's part of Jodi's caring nature and generosity of spirit. We might just talk about the latest updates, but if I'm facing a specific challenge, Jodi is the first person I call to talk it through.

Finding my voice

There have been many times when Jodi has guided me in making important decisions, but there are three pivotal moments that really stand out. In the first instance, I had been in a fairly junior role at the bank for a couple of years, felt I'd mastered it and was looking for the next step up. I wanted to be recognised for my achievements and contributions to the team and needed to have that conversation with my boss. Jodi was amazing. She coached me to stand up for myself and to confidently ask for recognition. Performance is the bottom line, but you've got to have the guts to make yourself known, and not be afraid to self-advocate. I clearly remember her saying, 'It's easy to be a hard worker, but there are lots of them in the bank so you need to ensure you are noticed.' So I prepared a presentation for my boss, outlining everything I had achieved, the KPIs I had met and exceeded, and the things I had done that enhanced the team's overall performance. I basically benchmarked myself against the rest of the team, to demonstrate that I was ready for a promotion. Asking for the promotion by proving I was ready made all the difference.

Just have the guts to give it a go

The next time Jodi hugely influenced my career was a few years later. I had got that promotion within my team and again felt I had plateaued and was wondering, 'What next?' I believed I was ready for another promotion but was unsure where to go or what to do. I spoke to Jodi at length during this time. I considered several options within ANZ, as well as outside the bank. Jodi urged me to get out of my comfort zone and to apply for the Generalist Bankers Program. Although this seemed like an incredible development opportunity, participating in this program required a commitment to work overseas for an extended period. I was in a long-term relationship with my partner (and future husband) and this opportunity would mean putting my career ahead of my personal life. That was never an option for me. I had been in a long-distance relationship before and it wasn't something I wanted to do again. Nevertheless, I recognised that in order for me to grow and become a better banker I needed to get out of my comfort zone. I applied for one role that I was very excited about, got to the final two on the short list and missed out. I remember becoming very frustrated as there were no other opportunities available, feeling stuck in a rut. I would ask Jodi: 'Why not me? Why wasn't I picked?' I think I was a little too impatient. And Jodi would reply: 'It's a long game. Just keep at it.' Around this time, a twelve-month opportunity came up in the equity capital markets team. It was an amazing opportunity for me to learn totally new skills in a completely new role so I went for it. The role had an element of risk in that it was a fixed term appointment to cover a maternity leave position, so there was no guarantee of a permanent role at the end of it. But I remember Jodi urging me to go for it and giving me the confidence to deal with whatever happens at the end.

What is the worst that can happen?

The third pivotal moment came twelve months later, at the end of this secondment. My boss wanted to keep me because I had been doing a great job, but there was no budget or headcount to keep me in the team. I felt like a homeless person without a position. I could have returned to my former role in my original team but I wasn't excited about going back to a role I felt I had grown out of. I was really at a crossroads. While I felt committed to the bank long term, I couldn't see an exciting future for me there. That is when I started to look outside the bank.

I'd been interested in information technology for some time and decided to google 'best technology company in the world to work for'. A company I had only vaguely heard of called Salesforce came up. I decided to apply for a job with them. I really didn't expect to get it because I had no experience in technology or engineering, but to my shock they came back with an offer. Around that time I also received an offer to work for a start-up firm in financial advisory services, as an equity partner. Then a great offer came up internally within the bank. Three opportunities all at once! I had to work through three distinct options: stay in my comfort zone in the bank; stay in financial services but move to a start-up with equity; or totally change my career path. ANZ's offer was great, and I was terrified about leaving behind everything I had built. The start-up sounded exciting and cool, but technology kept gripping me.

After much soul-searching with Jodi I decided to take the risk and move to Salesforce. She stressed that technology is the future and the opportunity to do something like this doesn't come around very often. 'What is the worst that can happen?' she asked me. For me, it's easy to lose perspective and think it will be the end of the world if something doesn't work out. Talking it through with Jodi, I realised that the banking sector will always be there for me if IT doesn't work out. I don't know if I'd have got myself over the line if it weren't for Jodi.

Life beyond the banking world

After leaving the bank, I thought Jodi wouldn't be interested in keeping in touch. 'Perhaps I'm dead to her,' I thought, but I soon received a message from Jodi just touching base, asking me how I was settling in. 'Oh my god, she remembers me!' was my first thought, how wonderful that our relationship can continue.

I'm now facing a whole new set of challenges and although Jodi doesn't have a background in technology, it's not subject matter or technical expertise I need from her.

> *I value her expertise with leadership and self-management skills such as influencing, working through problems and negotiation. Jodi has been fantastic in cheerleading for me—reminding me about the long game, encouraging me to keep going and giving me the tough feedback when I need it.*

I've been able to run some difficult scenarios past Jodi, and she has taught me how to deal with them professionally and unemotionally. In one case I was dealing with a manager who took a very aggressive approach to an issue I raised. Jodi taught me to hold my ground if

I believed I was right. She also encouraged me to look at it from this manager's perspective. Why was she behaving in this way? What doesn't she know? What do you need to get her to know and understand? Perhaps she misunderstood my intentions. One of her mantras is to always look at something from the other person's perspective.

Jodi also taught me how to take the emotion out of a difficult situation or conversation, and that I don't need to respond straight away. It's okay to take some time to think about the conversation and speak with the person in a couple of days. It's a great strategy that I've used many times since.

My advice to women is to proactively seek out a mentor for themselves, start a relationship and then listen to the different perspectives that a mentor can give. Also be very respectful of their time. Come prepared with something to discuss, take on board their advice and be willing to put their suggestions into practice. They really appreciate you coming back to them with feedback on what worked for you.

Mentoring has a special place in careers for women

Mentoring is especially important for younger women in male dominated industries like banking. It can be a real challenge for young women to succeed, especially when there are so few women role models in senior positions to show the way. Jodi has trail blazed her way up the career ladder, challenged institutional mindsets and gender stereotypes, and has been through so many experiences that I will inevitably face. Having access to her insights and experience is critical in preparing me for those situations and creating my own success.

Reflections

For mentors:

- What strategies could you use to ensure your highly ambitious mentees are progressing their careers at the right pace, and not missing out on learning opportunities by pursuing excessively rapid career moves?
- What can you share with other mentors around when and how to provide tough feedback to your mentee?
- Developing empathy is partly about seeing a point of view from the other person's perspective. How can you challenge your mentee to foster greater empathy?
- What are the biases, institutional mindsets and stereotypes women struggle with in your organisation?
- What is the role of men in mentoring women?

For mentees:

- Is your work going unnoticed? What steps have you taken in the last 6 months to promote your capabilities and achievements? What has been stopping you? What else could you do?
- Who are the people in your workplace outside your immediate reporting relationship that could sponsor you, advocate for you and advance your career? How can you demonstrate to them who you are and what you are capable of?
- What would you like to be known for in your organisation? How can you receive information about what you *are* known for? What is the gap between your desire and the reality? What strategies can you work on to close the gaps?
- When do you need to be pushed and challenged by your mentor? When do you need to be supported and nurtured?
- What is one courageous thing you can do to get out of your comfort zone and try something new?

The Yin and Yang of coaching women's football

◇◇◇◇◇

Chyloe Kurdas & Wayne Siekman
Australian Football Women's League (AFLW)

Chyloe Kurdas

Chyloe was the Australian Football League (AFL) Victoria's female Football Development Manager from 2007 to 2016. She has been the driving force behind the cultural change for the inclusion of women and girls in football in Victoria. Chyloe's strategic leadership helped to establish a record number of over 300 community-based female teams across Victoria. With the support of a number of hand-picked coaches she also established an under 18s (U18) high performance program for over 450 of Victoria's most promising female footballers. Chyloe has worked hard to demonstrate that Australian women have sufficient talent to support a vibrant national women's league. Her drive and commitment have been vital in convincing the AFL to commit to a national competition for women footballers and have revolutionised women's participation in football. The AFLW has since captivated Australia with sell-out crowds, exceptional TV ratings and captivating games. Chyloe is now an AFLW radio and television commentator and writes for ESPN as their AFLW columnist.

Wayne Siekman

In 2013, Wayne Siekman made a decision that changed his life. With sixteen years of coaching experience, including coaching the Dandenong Stingrays in the TAC (Transport Accident Commission) Cup and coaching the Victorian Metro Youth Girls to national championships, he decided to accept a role on the coaching panel of Collingwood's inaugural national women's league. He has never looked back.

Chyloe's story

Climbing that mountain

I see the emergence of the AFLW as a great example of a community-led, bottom up movement. Women's football has been influenced and developed over decades by parents who have daughters who played—and by the girls themselves—as well as club coaches and progressive community football clubs.

The AFL came on board with women's football around ten years ago, appointing people like me in each state who were charged with driving that community growth. I was playing in the Victorian Women's Football League (VWFL) at the time and took on this role after one too many knee injuries meant I had to shift from being a player to becoming a coach. Three years later, in 2010, the AFL committed to a national championship for women and this decision led me to re-evaluate my role. While I was a reasonable coach, I knew I wasn't a high-performance coach at that point, and felt I couldn't give the girls what they needed into the future. So I put myself back in the shoes of the athletes, and asked myself, 'If I was a player, what sort of coach would I want?' I set out to identify emerging male coaches who were looking for an opportunity to challenge themselves. I identified a succession of really good men who were coaching in the U18 TAC Cup developing our most promising male players.

I initially worked with people like Andrew Jago, who went on to coach Melbourne University's women's team in the VFL, to build the talent development program. We brought in assistants, psychologists and fitness coaches, then Paul Groves (current Western Bulldogs AFLW Head Coach) joined us. Wayne came along in 2013, when Paul was our head coach. Andrew and I created version 2.0 of the talent development program, then Wayne and I modified and improved on it, creating version 3.0.

I was appointed to set up grass roots programs so girls could play football at a local level. But that was as high as they could go in competitive football. I wasn't satisfied with that. I was more aspirational, and had a vision of creating a high-performance football pathway that would culminate in a national women's competition—providing girls with the same pathway to pursue their aspirations as boys. The journey felt a bit like climbing one mountain—state football—and then another mountain—the national competition.

We recognised very early on that we had to build talent that would warrant the AFL supporting a women's league. This is where the coaches came in. We couldn't have done it without guys like Andrew, Paul and Wayne. They had coached boys in the TAC Cup for many years, and provided the girls with the same level of quality coaching and leadership as the boys. Once the girls started playing well, the AFL stood up and took notice. They recognised that this was something they could package up and sell, and upon which they could build a national competition.

A new coaching model for girls

With my background in psychology and health promotion, I was conscious of providing a program that understands the needs of our female athletes. For instance, if a kid is underperforming or she's training poorly the first question we ask is: 'Is she okay?' as opposed to 'Gee, she's been annoying or training poorly tonight'. We know that teenage girls at different points in adolescence can be really self-focused, so they might have to be coached and managed differently as they get older. In twelve months' time, if we stick with them, they could be completely different.

Developing a relationship with girls is largely around building their confidence, their self-belief, and their self worth. Girls often have a growth mindset, they are open for growth because they are like sponges, always wanting to learn.

Players that have been playing for four or five years know they are good, but the new ones really struggle with building self-belief. Last night, for instance, I was coaching a new team and I said to them 'Put your hand up if you don't really think you're good enough to be here'. Every kid puts her hand up. 'Why did you get invited?' I asked. They said, 'We work hard'. I go 'Yep.' 'Someone sees something in us.' 'Yes.' Then someone eventually said, 'People think we've got a bit of a talent?' They always externalise their capability, it never comes from within themselves. We teach them self-belief because we believe that internal motivation and self-confidence is the platform from which you should operate. Almost every single AFLW player that has come from our U18 program didn't think she was good enough to be there when she first joined it.

Boys are different. They would say, 'I should be here'. They wouldn't feel comfortable putting their hand up and showing that they weren't confident.

So it's really important to appoint the right coach, who understands the differences between coaching boys and girls. They must have a nice balance of masculinity and femininity in how they coach and apply themselves. They've got to be process focussed, caring, tender, nurturing, loving and empathic. They've got to balance this with knowing when to be outcome and instruction-focused, knowing when it's right to raise their voice, or be very firm and concrete. They've got to know how to bring those two things into the coaching relationship, because female athletes often lack confidence.

Trust and love: the vital ingredients to success in the AFL Women's League

Having been a female athlete, I know the relationship with the coach is really special. When our coach sees something in us, we hang on to every word they say. We tend to expect women to be nurturing, caring and want to please others. That seeps into the way girls think and act, and the value that they place on relationships. We care about how our coach is feeling, so we don't want to let them down. It's in our wiring.

Wayne is a very caring guy, really loving. He feels his emotions, and he's a lover of people. That's really apparent in how he coaches the girls, whether they're U18s or adult women. Love and care are important factors in how we lead female athletes. Wayne's gifts are really well suited to the needs of the female football community.

Men's football is quite different. You need to motivate them differently, almost turn around and whack them and go 'That was a shit effort mate.' If you said that to a woman, she'd never come back. Although I have observed a shift towards a more loving and caring approach among some of the male coaches, so maybe a more balanced, nurturing way of coaching footballers will eventually seep into the coaching method in men's football too.

The ideal partnership—kindred spirits

Wayne and I have a great partnership. Although I was his boss, there was no real sense of a hierarchy, quite the opposite. Our relationship was very collaborative, and there was a real teamwork element to it.

> *I wanted the program to have a philosophy of growth—to be process oriented, packaging things up, ticking all the boxes and recruiting people, not just players, and Wayne had a similar approach. So we were like kindred spirits.*

We really complemented each other in terms of technical expertise too. Wayne would speak to the people in the football world that might not have been willing to listen to a female voice. Then, if we needed a female lead, I would speak to those people. I was also able to help Wayne understand the specific needs and motivations of women and girls, as well as teaching him how to manage same-sex attracted athletes. Last year we had to cut a girl from the grand final whose same-sex partner was in the leadership group. These are fifteen and sixteen-year-old girls. As a woman and as a same-sex attracted woman I've been able to mentor Wayne and the team about these dynamics,

It was also terrific for Wayne to bring in his knowledge of coaching in the TAC Cup for the last sixteen years. He would challenge my thinking with new ideas and push us to take the program one step further. I loved hearing him say 'I've got this great new idea. Could we do this? Could we find some money for that?' He taught me to be really open to new ideas.

A united purpose guides everything

We were on a journey together and it was about committing to developing the breadth and capability of our athletes over the long term, rather than focusing on winning the next game. That journey was tested at times, and led to what may have been some disappointing outcomes for Wayne, particularly in the first year. We lost a game where we had a deliberate strategy to play one of our best players across the centre half back role rather than through the middle. If we'd played her in the middle we would have won, but we were committed to developing this girl's footballing versatility. Now we've showcased her in the middle, we've showcased her up forward and we've showcased her down back. It's worked because now the league has got this amazing athlete as a result.

It was really important that Wayne didn't internalise that outcome as a personal failing on his part and that we didn't put him or the team in that position again. So, in 2015 we dedicated ourselves to implementing strategies to boost the performance of the players. Over the long term, it's paid off. The grand final this year was the most perfect game of football I've ever been involved with. It's the culmination of three years of working together, refining our relationship and the program we built together.

Having a mentee mentality

When you're the first in something, it's more challenging to find a mentor. I remember when I had my first knee injury and I didn't handle it well. It was all about me and my pain. I could have used someone like a mentor to tell me to roll my sleeves up. I needed someone to tell me to be selfless because my team needed me to focus on them and not on myself.

The closest person I had to a mentor was Grant Williams, former General Manager at AFL Victoria. When I worked with him, female football was really gaining a lot of momentum. His view was, 'We need to help Chyloe get even better at how she does things'. It wasn't about my output; it was about my process. I really appreciated that. Grant really influenced my approach to mentoring others, and even now I touch base with him.

I have a mentee mentality even if I don't have a dedicated mentor. I don't necessarily walk up to someone and ask, 'Can you mentor me?' but I'm always open to asking for information and receiving feedback from people whose opinions I value. With my career moving into the media, one of the first things I did was contact some people that had called games before.

The greatest lesson I've learned from Wayne is the importance of building relationships around trust and care. When you have those two things your potential is limitless—you can achieve anything you want.

Wayne's story

A career-changing decision

I came into the AFLW program in 2013, knowing very little about female football. It was very late in the piece—maybe six weeks out from the nationals—when Paul Groves approached me and asked if I'd like to get involved. They were looking for an assistant coach, and I jumped at the opportunity. At that stage the draft had been mostly completed, so most of the players were selected.

It was still a State-based game then. The role of coaches like me was to prepare the athletes for when the national opportunity came up. The head coach at the time was very hands-on and all the training and coaching plans were already set up. We just turned up and basically ran the drill for him. I was like an observer—which was good, because I could just come in and see things from afar. I gained a really good understanding of what should be done, which prepared me for when I was offered the opportunity to become the head coach six months later.

The hard road to success

Getting beaten for the first time in my first year was hard. Even though I accepted it, I was quite emotional after the game. You could see it in the girls as well. I moved on knowing that I'd coach again next year and that I had a really good starting base. Still, my friends and other people would joke around. 'You're the first coach to lose one. You're good, aren't ya?' You know that's going to happen because that's what your male mates say. You just cop it and move on.

The second year was about building up the program. We went to Perth and beat them on day one. It was a great win because Western Australia were the home town defending champions and favourites to win; the pressure was on them and they folded. Winning that game was pretty satisfying, and a lot more emotional than the previous year. To actually win the first game was very confirming.

All the hard work started to pay off. By the third year, I knew the players trusted what I had been saying, but even more importantly they would teach each other. That was a pivotal moment for me. We really didn't need coaches on grand final day. We could have just sat in the grandstand, and I have no doubt that the result would have been the same.

The excitingthing about coaching women's football right now is that it's all new and there's no definitive answer on how to coach. All the clubs are coaching differently and the competition in Victoria is quite close—no-one knows what's right or wrong yet.

Developing life skills

Creating a professional, national competition means that just teaching girls how to play football is not enough. We also need to teach them the habits of a professional, elite athlete—how to cope with the travel, play in hot conditions, quickly recover from fatigue, be flexible and adaptable. These girls are fourteen to seventeen-years-old, and they need to grow up fast. They need to learn how to cook, eat the right things, do the right recovery and look after themselves, so that when the AFL competition comes along they are prepared on all levels. With that level of preparation, you're more likely to pick girls who tick all the boxes and know what to do, over some thirty-year-old who only knows how to play the game.

It's really paying off. Psychologically, these girls are very well adjusted. I've seen some girls in other States, where they don't focus as much on life skills, really struggle by comparison.

What I love about this coaching role is that the female players are like sponges. They listen and observe everything you do. You have to be an extremely good role model, because they look to you to teach them everything—whether it's on the field or off the field. Teaching them habits that they're going to have to deal with when they become adults, even social time. They just absorb it and execute everything you say to the best of their ability. If it doesn't work it's because I stuffed the drill up, or I stuffed up the wording of it. It's never on them because they go and follow my instructions to a T.

What I've learned about women

Coaching U18 girls footy is different to coaching boys on so many fronts. Some of the boys have been playing footy for over ten years and they know how to play the game, they are conditioned for it. The girls, on the other hand, haven't had that opportunity. Before the national women's football league emerged, many of them had to stop playing once they turned fourteen-years-old, so they lost the game awareness. They are not physically conditioned in the way they would be if they had continued to play. I want them to learn the game as quickly as possible, but I understand it's going to take at least two to three years for the teams to improve their strength, their fitness, their speed, their skills and their game awareness.

But they're quick learners. I think women get it quicker than men. That's why women are smarter with most things; they absorb everything you say, and they will try and execute the best way to do it. That's massive. Males are often more inclined to say, 'I already know this.'

I have to be more aware of the girls' mental state when it comes to the drafting process. The AFLW is a shorter season, and the girls are only on six-month contracts. They'll react more emotionally if they get selected, or not selected, or are dropped and not playing. This emotional element plays into the selection process for me. I am more inclined to take girls who I think could be more resilient, often the older ones.

I learned a hard lesson about the different psychology of female players in my first year in the State league. We had played Queensland in one of the most fascinating games I've ever participated in. No-one scored a goal until about seven minutes to go, when Queensland got the first goal to put them in front. We responded within a minute, and kicked one just near the end to beat them. I remember the half-time of that game—that's the one and only time I gave them a spray. I yelled at them pretty harshly, to try and rev them up like I would do with the boys. The girls didn't really respond. That was only my second game as the head coach of a females' team. In the years since then, I have not had to yell at them like I would yell at the men. I've had to tell them off, but I've done it in a tone that was putting it back to them, not coming from me directly.

However, there are times when you need to coach them like blokes, and give them a spray, even if they feel uncomfortable about it. For instance, after the game in round two when we lost to Melbourne, we didn't just lose, we got destroyed after being twenty points up. I was hugely disappointed and felt I had to be very direct with them. The players didn't enjoy getting the tough message from me, but I know it's better hearing it from me first than from the real world out there. They are used to being the heroes right now, and haven't had to face harsh criticism yet. I said to them 'Now that you are on national TV, you're going to hear worse from other people. You're going to hear people saying things like "How could Collingwood lose that game after being twenty points up?" You girls just gave up.' It's about developing their resilience so they can cope with the negative public commentary that is bound to come their way.

Females are also different to males during the performance review process. I have found they will brood on one negative comment and forget about all the positive feedback I have given them. They have got to stop dwelling on them, take negative comments on board more, embrace the feedback, and do something about it.

My own mentoring journey

Gavin Brown and Alan Richardson were great mentors to me earlier in my career. They were establishing a Collingwood VFL team from scratch and my goal was to learn as much from them as possible so I could become a better coach. Seeing the two of them work behind the scenes helped me enormously. They gave me a better understanding of how I could teach U18 kids that were on the fringe of getting to that next level.

I've got other mentors who I can call up, like Graeme Yeats, who used to play for Melbourne and got me into coaching for the Stingrays for ten years. I still speak to him two or three times a week and still rely heavily on his support and advice. The way he gives feedback is more about having a joke and being a mate rather than a mentor, because I've known him for so long. Eighteen months ago I called him up and said, 'The Nationals are coming up. Any advice for me?' He went, 'I don't need to give you any advice. You know what you're doing. Just piss off'. Early in this season he saw me on the television and said, 'Your eyes looked like they were popping out of your head. You looked like a dill.' He was having a crack at me again, but I knew that was feedback for me to just be myself when someone's talking to me.

I'm a better person now

Coaching women has enabled me to test and develop my coaching skills to a new level. I've shown that I've got a decent football brain, that I've got good plans in place on the field, which the girls are executing. I make sure that I've got the coaching brain off the field as well, to build rapport and trust. Things don't always go as planned on the field, but if players trust that you have given them the ability to execute a play, they will find a way through.

> *When I get home at night, I'm more energetic because I just love being around women who help me improve as a person and as a coach.*

I'll be up at 6am the next morning buzzing, already planning for the next day or the next week. Whereas I'd sometimes come home from a male session and it's more like going through the motions. Then again, I recognise I've still got some way to go. If I'm at home and with my wife and I'm back to your typical male. I don't know why that is yet, but I'm still probably working that through.

Since the AFLW season is over, I miss Chyloe. Now it's just footy, footy, footy. I'm lucky to have been with her for four years learning together, building a working relationship as well as a personal relationship. She knew me back to front after twelve months, knew that I just craved coaching this side and craved wanting to be there to help these young players develop.

I'm a better person for having coached the women's league. I now have a greater awareness of the female perspective—how women think, how to motivate them. I understand how they are feeling simply by observing them when they walk in to training. If they need a bit of love, then I talk to them; if they're fine, I let them go.

I just want to keep giving and giving as much as I can.

Reflections

For mentors

- What specific issues might women face in your workplace that men may not encounter?
- Do you believe men and women are motivated differently? If so how would you mentor them differently?
- How might the sporting analogy apply in your workplace?
- Would you mentor a peer differently to a more junior mentee?
- How has mentoring changed you? Have you become a better person, or a better leader? If so, in what ways?

For mentees

- What are key challenges men have working with women?
- What are the key challenges women may have working with men?
- What might you learn from having a male mentor?
- How can you foster a daily mentee mentality?
- How do you respond to performance feedback? If you are someone who under values positive feedback and over accentuates the negative, what strategies can you use to develop a more balanced approach?

Nurturing the passion

◇◇◇◇◇

Cindy Briscoe & Tina Chawner

Commonwealth Department of Agriculture and Water Resources & PwC

Cindy Briscoe

Cindy has moved through an extraordinarily broad range of experiences in the Commonwealth public service. From her early days as an information technology graduate, she has worked her way through to project management, program management and law enforcement roles in immigration and border protection. It was in this role that she chaired the WILES mentoring program and where she met Tina. She is currently a Deputy Secretary in the Department of Agriculture and Water.

Tina Chawner

Tina carved out a highly successful public sector career in the United Kingdom before migrating to Australia. Selected out of thousands of graduate applicants for the UK's Her Majesty's Revenue and CustomsGraduate program, she was fast-tracked through the ranks, eventually landing senior leadership roles in communications for a mega-department spanning over 85,000 staff. After moving to Australia with her husband, Tina had to continue her career—with no networks. She is now a Senior Manager at PwC's The Difference, that empowers clients to create solutions through collaborative, creative problem solving.

Cindy's story

From IT to law enforcement and beyond

I have been privileged to have had a broad range of opportunities in my APS career. The Australian Public Service (APS) has provided me withso many different career opportunities. When I started as an IT graduate, I never imagined that I would end up in law enforcement as a sworn officer, as Deputy Commissioner of the Australian Border Force.

I was one of three women in my university course, and one of two that graduated—it was a very male dominated field. I spent a few years programming before I discovered that it wasn't really me, so I steered toward project management and business analysis. With a combination of technical skills and people skills, I got promoted reasonably quickly. I've had the opportunity to work in large and small organisations. In smaller organisations you get across the whole business and get to really make a difference, lead change and shape the workplace culture. In large organisations you appreciate the complexities of multiple agendas and roles, scale and geographic spread.

My most rewarding and challenging role to date was working in the Department of Immigration and Border Protection and the Australian Border Force, leading support for regional processing (in Nauru and Papua New Guinea) and Australia's Immigration Detention network. In this role I also led the 'stand up' of the Australian Border Force on 1 July 2015, and at this time I was sworn in as Deputy Commissioner of the Australian Border Force.

I am now a Deputy Secretary in the Department of Agriculture and Water Resources leading all of the corporate and enabling functions. This role has me back in a role where I have a broad influence over organisational change and culture.

Back in 1999 the Hon. Amanda Vanstone (former Minister for Justice and Customs) launched a mentoring program called WILES to encourage women to pursue senior careers in Australian law enforcement and regulatory services. She convinced the heads of several law enforcement agencies to financially back this program; in return, each contributing agency could nominate several high performing and high potential women as participants. These days, senior women in law enforcement don't raise as many eyebrows, but back then, the battle to recognise women in this field was fierce indeed. At WILES, we matched nominated mentors and mentees based on background similarities, and career development needs. That's how I met Tina.

The mentoring mirror

Straight away I could see Tina's huge potential. She was a bundle of energy, enthusiasm and passion. She showed great interest and curiosity when I spoke about the challenges with the changes involved in merging Customs and the Department of Immigration and Border Protection. I could see all sorts of opportunities in our department for someone like Tina but blatantly poaching a person I was mentoring was a boundary I was not prepared to cross. Instead, I put her in touch with a couple of key people in my department and elsewhere and let her take it from there. I was hoping that once she started meeting with other people and developing her own networks she would recognise that she had options beyond her Australian Taxation Office (ATO) role, which was only temporary.

As our conversations evolved, I could see some of Tina's dilemmas mirroring the way my own working life had started out. For instance, I recognised that Tina needed to get noticed beyond her immediate team and manager. She knew she was a good communications professional and was concerned that her success as a specialist could mean she would become pigeon-holed. I had been through that situation before and had to take deliberate steps to get noticed beyond my specialist role.

I dealt with this by applying for a job 'out of left field'. It was a job that would expand my horizons and also demonstrate my interest and desire to step 'up and out'. At the time, I was working in the Australian Tax Office and I applied to be the personal assistant to the Commissioner. I think it's fair to say he was surprised by my application, but also interested, keeping me in the running until the final two.

Although I wasn't selected, I did raise my profile. In fact, one of the Second Commissioners took the time to advocate for me for opportunities to show what broader contribution I could make.

Listening to Tina's struggles with finding her passion at work made me reflect on my own career journey, on instances when I let my own plans be overtaken by someone else's ideas of what they wanted me to do, rather than trust my own judgement. Tina struck me with her passion and plan, which is admirable, and in turn inspired me.

Mentoring is a great process of self-reflection. I know that the advice I give others is always a good reminder for myself. For instance, I often tell other women to reach out for help, which I'm still not very good at. I remember when one of my mentors offered to connect me with a colleague who could share her experience doing a 'big job' as a single parent. My first reaction was 'she's a Secretary of a Department, I can't just call her and ask her for coffee.' I did find the courage to call her, we met and we talked about managing caring responsibilities and work. Not only was it incredibly helpful given my own situation as a single parent in a high pressure role, it opened the door for future connections. Now I often say to other women 'Pick up the phone and call, what's the worst thing that can happen? It doesn't have to be anything more than a coffee and a chat. Tell them you're really interested to hear about what they're doing, or that you want to talk to them about some career options.'

As a senior leader it's really important to take time to reflect, yet often we are running at a million miles an hour and find it a struggle to stop. Being a mentor forces me to reflect on what I've learnt in my own career.

Success lies in the spontaneity of the relationship

I think I'd struggle to restrict any mentoring relationship to just a formal process. Tina and I started out meeting on a formal basis, but that soon changed to us meeting whenever she had a specific issue she wanted to discuss, or when she wanted help. You don't need a mentor on a certain day of the month every month. You need them when you need them, and it's often because you want to debrief about something, or you're thinking of applying for a job and it closes tomorrow, or you've got an application you want looked at, or you want to prepare for an interview. Not that formal mentoring programs don't work—after all, we met through the WILES mentoring program. It's just that forcing a process onto a mentoring relationship may kill the flow and spontaneity that's essential to success.

> *Our relationship flowed because we had a genuine connection. It's a bit like sitting down with strangers at a dinner party. Sometimes the conversation flows easily, other times there's just not that connection.*

Often it's about two people having similar values or approaches to life and work. Most people who reach out to a mentor do so because they see commonalities. Often women are attracted to me as a mentor because I'm a senior woman and a single parent. People will often say, 'Wow. That's even more challenging. How do you do that?' That's often the start of the conversation, then we get into other things—like the fact we've both worked in similar environments orthe challenges of working in law enforcement as a woman.

My passion and commitment

For me, mentoring is a passion and a commitment. Julia Gillard, Australia's first female Prime Minister, wrote: 'It's hard being a senior leader. Being a senior female leader has extra challenges. Being a senior female leader that's in the pursuit of greater diversity and gender balance in leadership is even harder still.' I often think about the truth in those words. There are not many female senior leaders in the Australian Public Service, and even fewer women who have the time and space to mentor and support other women.

I recently caught up with a woman who used to work for me, and has now moved to the private sector. I was curious about what she found useful in our relationship, so I asked her for feedback. ‘It’s hard to put my finger on it’, she said, ‘but it’s partly personality-based and the fact that I really like you as a person. We get on and I trust your judgement. You listen. I never feel like I’m going to be judged by you. You’re very generous with your time and you’re very genuine in your feedback.’ I guess that sums up the things that are important to me.

If you’re mentoring someone because it’s your job, I don’t think it works as well. Mentoring requires you to be generous and genuine, which won’t work if you consider it simply a duty or responsibility. You need to be generous in sharing your stories and making yourself available, even if it’s just a quick phone call. And you need to be genuinely listening, not judging.

Confidentiality is important too. At times you may want to discuss a difficult relationship or a difficult encounter, and in Canberra, there’s a good chance you will know the person or people being discussed. We work around these potential conflicts of interest by keeping names out of the discussion. If necessary, we also agree that a particular discussion needs to stay in the room. Either way, as the relationship is built on a strong foundation of trust, we know that whatever we share with each other will remain confidential.

I also think women are often more prone to being pigeon-holed in their careers than men, and this is important to explore when mentoring women. In my observation, men are given more chances to take up new or broader roles outside their area of expertise, whereas women tend to be offered the same types of roles and become specialised. This means that women like me have a special role as advocates for other women to ensure they are being considered for broader opportunities. Many women are not natural advocates for themselves and will hold themselves in check with persistent self-doubts about their capability. I’ve heard many women say: ‘That’s not me. I haven’t got the skills to do that.’ No matter our skills, capabilities and brilliance, this lack of self-confidence can be a real career blocker for women. I remember hearing the Hon. Michaelia

Cash, the Minister for Women saying, 'You've got to open doors for other women because often they won't open them for themselves.' She then went further, saying, 'When you're on a selection panel, if there aren't enough women in the field, go out and encourage some.'

I'm not the sort of person that can get up onstage and advocate for women's issues. I like to do it quietly at the ground level, on a personal level. People don't want advice from a deputy secretary or deputy commissioner, they want advice from a real person. As a mentor I offer myself as a real person with some experience that I can share with other women on an equal basis.

Tina's long term plan was to be in a position where she could help people make change, where she could influence, innovate and create, and she's achieved that plan. I'm so proud to have been part of her journey.

Tina's story

The wild ride

I started my career in England as a graduate for Her Majesty's Revenue and Customs (HMRC) on a management fast-track scheme. It was a massive scheme, with only ten people selected out of thousands of people applying each year. Each year for four years, we were rotated through different jobs and were provided with amazing support. We had a psychologist working with us every year, mentors and we were given a lot of feedback. It was fantastic, amazing and very confronting at times, and the experience was an incredible learning journey.

My first management role was in HMRC, which was my first exposure to managing culture clashes in the workplace. I then led a national strike force team of up to ten customs officers, a really tough job. Only two of the team were women, the rest were men. I remember my first day there, sitting around the table with all the other managers, all male and all around twice my age, wondering how this would pan out. But it did work out. There were some very tough, intimidating experiences, but I also learnt so much about the role of a Customs officer, how to manage teams and how to build relationships (particularly in a male dominated environment!).

I came into communications by being in the right place at the right time. I remember the day it happened very clearly. I was working in a team simplifying policy advice between HMRC and Her Majesty's Treasury when we lost a disk that contained sensitive child benefit data. It was a massive event,and it led to the CEO resigning. The first we knew about it was when we saw it on the BBC News. There were News cameras everywhere, and we had to exit the building surrounded by cameras and police. The Department needed a strong manager to lead the IT communications team through this crisis. Although I had no communications background, I felt I had the management experience and so I agreed to take up the opportunity. It was a baptism of fire. I was leading a team of people who didn't want to be in communications, and we were constantly being bombarded with media requests. I loved it and I thrived. I was then asked to lead the Department's Change Communications, involving 85,000 staff.That was another amazing challenge.

During this time my husband, who is Australian, wanted to return home. We said goodbye to all our friends and our entire network in the UK and migrated to Melbourne. It was tough coming to Australia. Although we had my husband's family and friends, I had lost my strong network and I was at somewhat of a loss for the first twelve months. I began working with a consulting firm but soon felt I didn't really fit into the culture. I applied for a role with the Tax Practitioner's Board, assuming the role was based in Melbourne. The same day we were going to purchase a house in Melbourne, the Board contacted me and told me the Chair really wanted me for the role, which was based in Canberra. Initially I wasn't interested, but after a lot of convincing, the job sounded just too good to refuse. So we decided to make another move, where we knew nobody.

After eighteen months, another opportunity came up and I

accepted another role at the Australian Taxation Office (ATO) where I participated in the WILES mentoring program. My managers recognised my capability and potential, so they nominated me for the program as part of my professional development.

What I learned from my mentor

The WILES program had an established process and structured set of activities over a twelve month period, before evolving into a more informal relationship. It was a significant time for me. My husband and I wanted to start a family and I was nervous about how this would impact my career, I felt I was ready for a new role and challenge, and at the same time I felt settled for the first time since arriving in Australia.

A major turning point came for me very early on in the program. We were asked to prepare a pyramid of all the elements in our life and work that are most important to us—things like learning new skills, and making a difference. We then had to reconstruct the pyramid into the way we currently experience our role. It struck me that what I was trying to achieve in life and in my career just didn't match the job I was in. I remember sitting down with Cindy and asking, 'What the hell am I doing here? I want to be making more of a difference.' That was a real moment of truth. That's how our mentoring conversations began, and they progressed from there.

By identifying my passions, Cindy and I were able to work on three specific challenges, all of which overlapped. First, we sorted through my work and family priorities, as I was considering having children. Listening to Cindy about how she had brought up two girls, while in pressured and senior positions was incredibly reassuing and insightful. Secondly, I felt my career was stagnating and I was grappling with how to break beyond my skill set as a communications specialist. Thirdly, I was struggling with the choice of staying in government or moving into the private sector. Through sharing her own experiences and testing my thinking on all these fronts, Cindy helped me understand all the implications so I could make informed and confident decisions.

Cindy also enabled me to connect with other people, so my network instantly became larger. I had an enormous network in the UK, but when I came to Canberra I found it really difficult to break into the government system. When you work in a massive government department like the ATO it's easy to feel lost, invisible and stuck. Having a network of people outside the department helped me understand that I have options. I remember going for coffee with one woman Cindy introduced me to. She had so much energy and new ways of thinking about things that I immediately began learning and growing.

Cindy was there for me at one of the lowest points in my career, when I was crushed when I wasn't appointed to a role I really passionately wanted. I felt it was a job where I could really make a difference, and missing out on that opportunity meant I had no idea what to do next. Cindy was the first person I contacted. I called her because she was neutral, but I felt she understood the environment and what I was going through. She helped me process my emotions, and gave me some very frank, honest and open feedback that I would have had difficulty accepting from someone else. That was a really important conversation for me.

Drivers of success

Cindy and I are a good match because our backgrounds are so similar. Cindy previously worked in tax, so there are so many experiences I had that she can instantly relate to. She had also managed to raise children while having a successful career, and I was at just that point in my life. Sharing with Cindy the dilemma around trying to change career paths, but at the same time have successful home life, meant the world to me.

I was incredibly lucky having a mentor who could relate to me from day one. She created a great rapport by being open, listening and just being an objective, independent sounding board. I was always reassured when she shared that she had faced similar situations, and discussed how she approached them. I remember her saying to me, 'If you need me for anything just call.' From the very first meeting I felt comfortable sharing personal confidences with her. In fact, Cindy was the first person I confided in at work that I was pregnant.

Cindy is a great role model for me. By discussing her experiences and how she leads her team, she demonstrates how to be a successful female leader.

My anchor—making a difference

Cindy has challenged my thinking and made me look at my career journey beyond the workplace—taking in the whole picture of family life as well. That was massive.

For instance, after I returned from maternity leave it would have been easy to simply cruise in my current role. I know that my manager wanted to keep me in his team and kept offering me jobs in his area, but they didn't seem to offer the right challenge. I wanted to be given a problem I could get my teeth stuck into—run a hundred miles an hour with—many people said to me 'Being a new mum, you'll really want to take it steady, you won't want a full-time demanding job.' I remember thinking, 'And where does my passion go?' Other people also suggested staying where I was. 'Moving to the private sector after having a child would be the totally wrong thing to do,' I was repeatedly told. 'You'll be working long hours, have no home life and will have to travel a lot.' However, I needed to regain my passion for work, and just couldn't find it doing the same work over and over. It was good to have Cindy, who was objective and independent. She helped build my confidence so that when the PwC opportunity came along, I was able to negotiate the role's conditions. I remember being very open with the Partner here telling him, 'I have a six-month old baby at home. I can't travel and I can only work four days per week.' He was great. We discussed the role, how we could make it work and he agreed to the conditions.

The PwC team have been incredibly supportive. They always check in on me to make sure I'm okay, like last week when my husband had to travel interstate for work. I've only travelled overnight once in the last twelve months, and they are really respectful of my time when I'm not in the office. I've personally regained my energy, and have found that I'm growing professionally. I'm learning about how collaborative design works, and I'm still able to bring in my communications expertise as well. I feel like I can make a huge amount of difference to clients.

My mentoring relationship with Cindy has enabled me to feel comfortable and confident to say it's actually okay to have a family and still have a successful career. Apart from the PwC Partner who works in the practice area, none of the team members have children, so they will frequently suggest we go out for dinner or drinks. I now feel comfortable saying I need to go home. That's really important for me.

If there is one piece of advice I would give to first-time mentees, it's to be really open-minded and honest. If you don't feel like you can be open and honest, then you probably don't have the right mentor. It's also very important for you to prepare. Spend time before your meeting thinking about what you want to get out of your mentor, and then make time available afterwards to reflect on the conversation.

> *My mentoring relationship with Cindy has been instrumental in enabling me to establish critical business networks and stand out in the Canberra business community. It has transformed my career.*

If I didn't have the mentoring relationship, I think I would probably still be in the public service, not realising that it was the wrong career choice for me at that point in time. I have now regained my self-belief, have rediscovered my purpose and am connected with a wonderful network of colleagues and friends. I know Cindy will always be there for me, and we will always stay in touch.

Reflections

For mentors

- What dilemmas and challenges are your mentee facing that may mirror some of your own life experiences? Which of your personal experiences would be most powerful to share with your mentee? How do you remain objective in these situations?
- What advice do you give your mentee that you should probably apply to yourself?
- How can you build a process of self-reflection into your mentoring style to improve your personal effectiveness?
- How can you use your networks to help your mentee build her own networks?
- As the more senior person in a mentoring relationship it may be easy to fall into the trap of becoming patronizing or superior. How can you foster a relationship of mutual respect and equality so that you learn from each other?

For mentees

- What is your life's purpose? To what extent are you able to live your purpose at work? What obstacles are you facing to achieving this? What is one strategy you can adopt to live your purpose more completely?
- What are your passions? How can you live your passions at work?
- What are two or three key aspects of your working life you would like to change, to express your passion more fully?
- Do you have a network that is vertical (upwards focused) and horizontal (peer-focused)? What is your networking strategy? What are three steps you could take to increase your networks within your workplace and more broadly in your industry?

Mentoring through the generations

◇◇◇◇◇

Professor Carol Pollock,
Associate Professor Usha Panchapakesan
& Dr. Sarah Glastras

Royal North Shore Hospital, Sydney
University of Sydney

Professor Carol Pollock

Carol is a nephrologist at the Royal North Shore Hospital in Sydney. She is among a handful of iconic women who carved out successful careers as medical specialists during the 1980s. Throughout her career, Carol has had access to some of the most significant leaders in her field, many of whom were passionate about advancing women in medicine. She is now committed to helping the next generation of younger women break through the still male-dominated medical world.

Carol's former PhD candidates, Usha and Sarah, each took different career directions at the conclusion of their doctorates. Usha chose a career in medical research, while Sarah went on to work in clinical research and clinical practice.

Associate Professor Usha Panchapakesa and Dr. Sarah Glastras

Usha is a renal specialist at the University of Sydney Medical School. Her area of expertise concerns the renal complications of *diabetes mellitus,* with a specific focus in novel therapies.

Sarah is a staff specialist in endocrinology at Royal North Shore Hospital, and a consultant endocrinologist in private practice. Carol's support and mentorship has been integral to both these women's careers, and they consider Carol to be one of the most important forces in their lives.

Carol's story

The cycle of mentoring

My experience with mentoring has been more like a cycle, where women support each other, rather than an individual mentoring relationship. The cycle started with Dr. Priscilla Kincaid-Smith. She wasn't a formal mentor to me, but was someone who I held in very high esteem; a role model and real trailblazer for women in science.[1] Priscilla had a large family, and a very successful career at the highest level. She started the Australian and New Zealand Society of Nephrology back in the late 1950s with about four or five men. In the early 1960s, she was the first female president of the International Society of Nephrology. She was a real ground breaker and an icon for many women, including me. She led me to believe that it's possible for a woman to be a highly successful nephrologist, without sacrificing family or relationships. Priscilla's success made way for the next generation of dedicated and passionate women in medicine, including Judy Whitworth[2] who became my mentor.

As a mother with a stellar career, Priscilla was the exception in the medical profession. Before her, women who excelled in medicine had to be very single-minded and totally focused on their career—especially in surgery and medical physician roles. As a result, most women who made it in the profession associated achievement with doing it tough and making it on their own. Many didn't see why they should give a hand up to other women, especially since they'd had to fight so hard. This attitude created the notion that women must go through a 'rite of passage' before they can claim their hard-earned place in the medical world. Paradoxically, this meant that women were often harder on other women than on men. In that work environment, mentoring was not readily available to women. So, I was fortunate to have so many mentors.

John Mahony mentored me early in my career. He was my boss when I was an intern and junior doctor. John was a brilliant doctor for a lot of reasons—not just because of his expertise, but also because of his human qualities, which endeared him to his patients. He was also somebody who successfully juggled career and a family—he had about eight or nine kids! John encouraged us to openly discuss difficulties at work. He was not afraid to share that he'd had a really bad day, and was upset over something. Through his actions, he demonstrated that it was okay to admit to being in a struggle. This went against the stereotype in the medical profession, where admitting to problems was seen as a sign of weakness.

John was somebody that I'd ring up and ask about clinical problems, as well as life issues. I remember his advice and guidance when I was pregnant. I was the first person in New South Wales to have a baby as a clinical academic, and I needed his advice about how I could continue working while being a mother. The University provided maternity leave, but the hospital sector told me they wouldn't provide it. I just accepted this as fact, until about three months later when I received a call from one of my colleagues who had also been denied maternity leave. Taking a stand on maternity leave rights meant I had to take on the hospital *and* the department. As a very junior doctor, I felt pretty anxious about it, and thought it might kill my career. I needed somebody like John to tell me it was the right thing to do.

I also considered my PhD supervisor, Michael Field, a mentor. He is much closer in age than the others in my mentoring circle; they were about a generation older. Over the thirty years we've known each other, we have developed a deep friendship. Michael was the kind of person to give me very frank advice. Sometimes I took it and sometimes I didn't, but I always knew that he was thinking about my best interests. On one occasion, I was irritated by his suggestion that I dress with more 'gravitas'. I wouldn't say I dress flamboyantly, but I don't wear the expected business attire. I thought, 'Well, I'm not going to change the way I present myself!' It was well meaning of course, but fell flat.

Although I can advocate effectively for myself, Michael did actively support me at a critical juncture. When I applied for a promotion to a professor position, I was only thirty-nine and everybody said I was too young. Michael made a presentation to the academic committee, urging them to consider my ability to meet the selection criteria and to not exclude me because of my age. I'm sure his support helped me secure the professorship.

Judy Whitworth was a more formal mentor for me than either John or Michael. Our relationship was quite structured, and would generally revolve around issues of promotion and job opportunities. Judy's mentorship was particularly important to me when I was considering shifting from clinical work in nephrology to more of a leadership focus. Judy had made quite a significant leadership shift herself, moving into the role of Executive Director of the John Curtin School of Medical Research, then the Chief Medical Officer of Australia, before leading a lot of work for the World Health Organisation (WHO). So, her insights were invaluable.

Because of the diversity in my circle of mentors, each one was critically important at different times in my life. Each of them helped to shape my most pivotal decisions. I decided on renal medicine because of John. Because I knew of Priscilla, I decided to specialise in nephrology. Michael and I have very different personalities, so he provides me with a unique perspective on issues that I may not have considered. Perhaps my experience has been more about learning from role models. I tend to follow the career paths of people who I admire, taking what I liked out of people's approaches and adopt them for myself. That has worked well for me.

The mentor in me

For the most part, I've been more of a mentor than a mentee. Currently, I supervise and mentor at least six PhD students. I also co-supervise a number of others, which also takes up a large amount of my time.

I have a large research laboratory—and am known as a very family friendly PhD supervisor—so I tend to attract students with young families. At one point, I could have had a crèche in my laboratory!

PhD supervisors are also mentors, because they inevitably teach students life skills. Completing a PhD is a rather raw process, and a fairly emotional experience. It is a highly stressful period, and all the things you don't like about yourself can come to the surface. Sometimes I feel like I'm the priest that most people don't have these days. Candidates might burst into tears over something, perhaps because of tension in the laboratory, or people just don't get along and treat each other disrespectfully. Teaching candidates to be more respectful or tolerant isn't part of a PhD per se, but it is an important life skill that is crucial in the workplace.

> *If the relationship between supervisor and student doesn't work, the PhD will be a nightmare for everyone. I make my candidates aware that our relationship is the key to a successful PhD; as such, I usually end up being long term friends with many of my students.*

My PhD students nominated me for the Vice Chancellor Award for PhD supervision in 2012, which values the concept of holistic mentoring.

I also participate in a range of external mentoring programs: one for junior female staff at the Royal North Shore Hospital, the Women in Medicine mentoring program in the hospital, and a mentoring program at Sydney University. I've been allocated two young women whom I meet with monthly over a coffee. I also have a more structured mentoring relationship with a pharmacist.

Confidentiality and mutual respect are my two ingredients for a successful mentoring relationship. Mutual respect is about starting from a place of equality and recognising that your mentee's view is as equally valid as yours. If you take an attitude that you are more senior and superior, your mentee could look up to you and conclude she could never be like you. You end up undermining her confidence about her ability to progress, the very reasons why you became a mentor in the first place.

What I've learned from my mentees

The medical profession in the 1980s was largely male dominated. Men occupied the senior roles and women the junior roles, and at every promotion opportunity, the number of women dropped off. In some ways, I think I was the recipient of positive discrimination—in the right place at the right time. I went through my career thinking female inequality wasn't a huge issue, but when I talk to young women in the Women's Society at North Shore, I realise I was mistaken. They clearly feel that there's a covert level of discrimination; they still take the lion's share of juggling the domestic and non-domestic side of life, compared to their equally busy husbands or partners. This means taking time off or working flexibly around family needs falls disproportionately on their shoulders, and is often not appreciated in the medical profession.

My mentees have given me a greater understanding of how different personalities respond to stress. I consider it a privilege when people honestly share their concerns with me. I allow them to bare their fears and concerns, without judgment. Sometimes friends are not the best person to confide in when you want to download, as they can be more inclined to judge.

Today there are so many more women in senior roles that gender equality is starting to become the norm. Hopefully, we will get to a point where women's aspirations for their personal and professional lives can be both met and not compete with each other.

Usha's story

I met Carol when i decided to undertake a PhD after qualifying as a kidney specialist. Carol was one of the best renal researchers, and had a great lab in my field of interest—diabetic kidney disease.

I was in clinical practice at St George's hospital, and one of the consultants at the hospital urged me to make contact with her. I kept running out of time, so my colleague actually called her and got me a meeting time. So that's how it happened.

Carol became my supervisor but our relationship quickly evolved into so much more than a clinical partnership. I was struggling with my sister's death from cancer, and around that time my first pregnancy didn't work out. Carol was so understanding when I was struggling with my personal issues. That made it a really deep and special relationship. She was also there for me in practical ways—like appointing a research assistant to help me when I physically couldn't manage the work, or having a colleague present on my behalf at conferences. I don't think I would have had such a successful PhD outcome without Carol's close personal friendship and support.

After completing my PhD, I decided to pursue full time research rather than returning to clinical practice. My relationship with Carol continued, although it shifted to a more intellectual level. We would have conversations about where the science was heading, and the cutting-edge areas in which she suggested I should invest. Through these insights, Carol helped me secure research grants, which enabled me to become an independent researcher with my own views and my own laboratory of researchers. Our skills gradually became more complementary and we started to work as a team—writing and reviewing papers, and supervising students together. These days, she helps me mostly with industry matters and community engagement.

Our personalities are quite different, and that balances us out. Carol is very positive person, believing anything is possible and that all obstacles can be overcome. I tend to see problems rather than seeing opportunities. She's a risk taker and I'm more conservative. It helps to have somebody look at situations in a different way. One of her mantras is that nothing is ever too hard. She never gives up. Together, we always find a solution. I've really benefited from her positivity and can-do approach, and she perhaps takes on board my realism when it is warranted.

Our values are also very different. Work-life balance is extremely important for me now, although it wasn't always like that. Before I started a family, I used to work around the clock. My job was all I had, and I would go home only after my work finished. Even then, I would still read journals and up-skill myself late into the evenings. But once I started having a family, it became really important for me to go home in the evenings to sit down for dinner with the children and get involved in their lives. My choice to focus on my family has definitely affected my career success. I'm not prepared to get involved in extra work-related commitments, such as volunteering for working parties or travelling to present at conferences. This has impacted my track record and my success as a leader in my field, but I make these trade-offs willingly.

Carol can juggle a lot of things and not feel stressed. She has managed her work-life balance very successfully and it seems effortless with her. Carol has also taught me to be more patient. I'm extremely impatient, and get easily frustrated when something is taking too long. I'm very concise and quick in my thinking, speaking and writing. Carol has endless patience, and her example has enabled me to learn more patience too.

I remember a well-meaning consultant warning me of the extreme workload that comes with trying to be as successful as Carol. But Carol has never expected anyone to follow in her footsteps, so we have a very good working relationship. I'm smart enough and mature enough now to know who I am, and I don't try to emulate her. There has never been any clash in expectations or judgements about each other's values or choices in life. There's only ever been mutual respect and understanding. With Carol there is so much room for me to be my authentic self.

I've been inspired to be a good mentor because of Carol's example. I often reflect on times when it was difficult for me, and how generously and kindly Carol treated me. I never felt I was taking up her time or troubling her. I strive to give others that kind of support and comfort.

> *Mentoring relationships should emerge naturally. They should be open, free and unbound by rules. I think it's important to have more than one mentor, including mentors in areas beyond your field of work so that there's no conflict of interest.*

I think it's important to appreciate a person can have different mentors at different stages of their life.

Sarah's story

I had known of Carol's awesome reputation for many years, but the pivotal moment came in 2012, when I was considering doing a PhD. A great mentor of mine, Professor Greg Fulcher, suggested Carol as a primary supervisor. I remember Greg calling Carol and she hot-trotted over to his office. We sat there and tossed around all the ideas that could be put into the PhD for the following year.

Carol knew all about how to succeed with a PhD. She knew about the possible pitfalls and the need to have back-up plans, which gave my grand ideas of clinical research some context. Despite not knowing me that well, she became my biggest advocate and wrote amazing references for my scholarship application for a prestigious NHMRC scholarship, which I was fortunate to secure.

Soon after Carol agreed to be my supervisor, I dropped a bombshell on her: I was pregnant with twins. She was just delighted, and told me, 'You do what you need to do. We can defer any scholarship you get.' She then said something that has always stayed with me: 'You know what? My experience tells me that it doesn't matter what a person is up against, it means nothing in terms of their capability. Sometimes people who have the most going on are the people who do the best.' So that was two steps forward for me, and I never looked back. I started the following year, and it worked out beautifully.

I was in a somewhat unique situation, because I needed to return to clinical practice part-time for financial reasons, while also completing my PhD. Carol knew how important it was for me to have financial security, and so actively supported my efforts to build up clinical practice. She even referred patients to me. That was pretty special, because in the PhD world mentors and supervisors usually don't like you taking on clinical work alongside your PhD.

During this time, I applied for a part-time staff specialist role in the hospital. I was still quite junior, so it was a substantial jump for me. Yet several senior people encouraged me to apply, assuring me that I was perfect for the role and I would have a high chance of success. I didn't get the role. Naturally, I was pretty cut up about it. Carol was there for me, and pulled me out of my disillusionment. Because of her level of seniority, she understood the way people work, the politics of the situation and how decisions are made. She reassured me that everything was going to be fine. I remember her saying 'This is one moment in your career. Something else will come up.' And it did. The following year while I was still completing my PhD, another role came up and I got it.

Jumping a high bar as a woman

The rite of passage is a very strong concept in the medical profession, and it's a real blocker for many women. Much of the medical profession has this ingrained attitude that younger people have to do it tough. I remember being about six months into my second pregnancy when I was doing overnight shift work in the hospital. I was so nauseous, vomiting for a lot of the time whilst I was on-shift. I got no compassion from my supervisors, including the women, whose basic attitude was 'Just get on with it. Suck it up.'

The dilemma of having children while forging a career is a real burden for women in medicine. There is an assumption that if you have children, you're not in it for the long haul and you're not going to be on the top of your game. And it's not just older men who are inflexible when it comes to accommodating your needs as a parent. If women haven't gone down that path of having a family themselves, they can be your worst enemy. Several of my friends have given up the specialist career path after having children because it has been too hard to fight those attitudes. Men can have children and there's none of that overtone around it being a career stopper.

With Carol I never felt that parental burden. Throughout my PhD I was renovating the house, having twins and raising two older children, applying for jobs and none of that made a difference to her view of my capability and potential. Carol has always allowed me to take the lead and is totally flexible with how I deliver my work. She would even find alternative ways around a situation if I couldn't be there for family reasons.

Carol is always available. I can send her something at the most God-forsaken hour and get a response by the morning. And she is so accommodating. She'll be on a plane to Spain or at some symposium and still find time to read my PhD and give me good feedback. That's going over and above what you would expect of a mentor.

What I really love about Carol is that she's so real and so honest. She's got a great attitude to life, particularly around making time for family. I always get an honest opinion from her. If she thinks something's not really going to work she won't stop me, but she'll give me her honest viewpoint.

Must-know lessons from Carol

Carol taught me so much about being a good mentor because she is such a fantastic role model herself.

> *Like her, I'm very flexible with my students because I understand their situations and know how important it is to have a supportive mentor.*

She also taught me to not have preconceived ideas about somebody's capacity, and to treat people you're supervising with respect and friendship—like a collegial relationship rather than a hierarchical approach.

The best advice I can give first time mentees is to choose a fabulous supervisor like Carol. You can look at someone's publication and supervision track record, but it doesn't take into account their personality and philosophies on life and careers.

1 Dr. Kincaid-Smith was a world-renowned nephrologist and a trailblazer for Australian female scientists. One of her most important discoveries was identifying the link between the overuse of headache powders Bex and Vincents and kidney disease in the early 1960s and in so doing saved countless lives. She had many firsts—she was the first female professor at the University of Melbourne in 1975, first female chair of the Royal Australasian College of Physicians, first female chair of the Australian Medical Association and the first female chair of the World Medical Association. (www.abc.net.au/news/2015-07-21/trailblazing-female-scientist-priscilla-kincaid-smith-remembered/6637276)

2 Professor Judith Whitworth, AC is the Director of The John Curtin School of Medical Research and Howard Florey Professor of Medical Research at The Australian National University in Canberra and heads the High Blood Pressure Research Unit. Professor Whitworth is an Ambassador for Canberra and an Ambassador for Women. She was Telstra ACT Business Woman of the Year in 2002 and 2004 ACT Australian of the Year. (www.acrf.com.au/bio-prof-judith-whitworth/)

Reflections

For mentors

- Are you part of a generation of mentors?
- Which mentors have inspired you?
- What have you learned from your mentors that you can pass on to the next generation of mentees?
- Have you experienced a culture where women are not supported by other women? How can you as a leader and mentor begin to change that behaviour?
- As a leader and mentor how can you begin to break down barriers and open opportunities across genders?

For mentees

- Would you benefit from being mentored by more than one person? How would you go about developing this network of mentors?
- What are the workplace cultural barriers that inhibit your ability to move sideways or upwards? How can you work through these barriers with your mentor?
- Does your workplace have a 'rite of passage'? How would you describe it? Which elements are you experiencing?
- What differences have you observed in your mentor's approach to life, and his or her values and passions, that you can learn from?
- How can you become part of a generational approach to mentoring? What are the most compelling lessons youreceived from your mentoring relationship that you can pass on to the next generation of mentees?

Don't worry, I've got your back

◇◇◇◇◇

Jerril Rechter & Bec Reid
VicHealth

Jerril Rechter

Jerril is Chief Executive of Victorian Health Promotion Foundation (VicHealth). In 1992, she founded the Launceston-based Stompin—a contemporary dance company focused on connecting young people in regional Tasmania through dance. Jerril met Bec Reid twenty years ago, when Bec was a sixteen-year-old dancer with a dream to join Stompin.[1] Throughout her career, Jerril has remained committed to promoting the arts as a vehicle through which people can explore their place in society. She has passed this belief on to Bec, and has proudly watched her find her own voice through artistic work and connection to the community.

Bec Reid

Bec began her artistic career as a dancer before taking on an enormous range of roles, including producer, director, choreographer, artistic director, and engagement specialist. She is also a Board member on various arts boards, collaborating with communities and artists nationally and globally. Bec lives what some might call the classic life of a millennial. From Footscray one week, to France the next, she could be anywhere on the world stage at any time. She now mentors young and emerging artists, applying the lessons she learned from Jerril. She got out of bed in her Hamburg hotel at 2am to share her experiences.

Jerril's story

A relationship born from a creative space

I can still remember the first time I saw Bec at the Launceston College Dance Studio. Stompin was holding an audition, and when Bec came into the room I was just gobsmacked. Bec came up to me afterwards, exuberant and gushing: 'Oh my God, I would love nothing more than to be involved in Stompin.

I saw qualities in Bec that clearly aligned to my own values and how I liked to live my life. That recognition was the basis for our deep connection, and the relationship grew from there. We are both driven by the values of community and social inclusion, that everybody has a place in society. Stompin is very much about connecting the Launceston community with artistic works, and finding out what's important to them. From the outset, Bec understood this vision. It's a vision which has guided all her decisions about creating an artistic career and working life ever since. This lifestyle choice is all-consuming. I'm not sure Bec has got the balance right, between her artistic work and her personal life, even today. I wonder where she finds time for herself. It's something I feel a sense of responsibility for, having guided her career journey.

The first real moment in our mentoring relationship came when I decided to leave Stompin. I had created the company, and had spent ten years developing it. It was like my baby, but it got to a point where I needed to move on and explore something else. I felt I was getting too old to lead the company, and that it needed some amazing, bright, young thing to take it to the next level. I was absolutely convinced that Bec was the type of person who could take Stompin where it needed to go. I trusted her vision and I trusted her practice. That realisation was a pivotal moment for me.

I asked Bec if she would be interested in taking on joint artistic directorship of the dance company along with Luke George, another young dancer. 'I'm not abandoning you', I assured her, 'I'll be on the board for a few years and I'll be your support. I'll have your back.'

The next generation leadership

When Bec and Luke started, the board were trying to adjust to having two new artistic directors. I was working with Bec and Luke, but also with the rest of the board to help them through the transition. There was also a young executive producer who formed the other part of the leadership team, and she too was challenged with how to work with two directors. I spent a lot of time trying to be that light touch to keep everybody going in the right direction.

Bec and Luke astounded me. They wrote this incredible triennial application that set up the company for the next period under their directorship. It was phenomenal. Writing a triennial is as intense and complex as writing a PhD and they pulled it off in their first year.

The leadership transition took around three years to complete. By then, Bec and Luke were flying. The work was absolutely brilliant, and the shows were critically successful. The board were happy and the momentum was there. Bec and Luke took it to a place that I couldn't have done.

Letting go

I remember when Bec made the decision to leave Stompin. It took me back to my own decision to leave, and brought back all the feelings that I had at that time. There is something about Launceston and Tasmania. Everyone knows you, it's all consuming, and it's powerful, but it does get to a point where you can't breathe. There's no break from work, no sense of personal space or life balance outside work and career. Knowing what Bec was going through, I just wanted to be there to support her however I could.

Stompin is hugely successful even now, and has gone from strength to strength. It's an astonishing legacy for me. It's grown, evolved, and changed over the last twenty-five years, but it is a very unique piece of artistic infrastructure. I think it can possibly only happen in Launceston. The community has grown up with the company, and everyone understands it innately. It's for the young, it's for the old. One of the dancers even has a tattoo of the dance company logo on her arm. She says Stompin saved her life. It's pretty powerful stuff. It's an amazing thing that all of us feel very proud of.

My unofficial board of mentors

Bec's practice is so honed and crafted. What I like to do is take leadership as my creative pursuit. I think the skill of being a leader is the most creative thing I do. I absolutely love it and I don't need to be in an arts context to be creative. But for Bec, her practice is who she is and it's how she thinks about the world. She is right at the forefront of contemporary practice in Australia, and internationally.

> *Because Bec has evolved her practice so much, I have actually leaned on her for her sensibility and guidance.*

She is definitely on my unofficial board of mentors. I'm not sure whether she knows it, but Bec is one of the few people with whom I can have creative discussions. She simply asks me questions back, as if she is *my* mentor.

It's incredibly important to have conversations offline, particularly in this role where the stakes are so high and you want to succeed. I trust Bec's judgement, because she's always got her eye on culture, on the issues and challenges facing the community and how the arts can help build social inclusion. Bec is one of the few people that actually know what's going on, on the ground.

With Bec and the other women and men I mentor, I don't see myself as some wise person imparting my knowledge down to them. I see it as more of an equal relationship—I seek Bec's guidance and counsel as much as I give it to her. There's a lovely reciprocity in our relationship, and we always come up with a better result when we work together.

There are two examples where this has happened. The first one was around ten years ago, when I was artistic director at the Footscray Community Arts Centre. I needed someone like Bec to work with the community on a developing clear artistic vision, so I convinced her to join me. At the time Footscray was quite an old, traditional community art centre, and we were trying to get it to adopt a more vibrant and dynamic practice; a place in the western suburbs that was contemporary and could hold its place artistically across the nation. I had absolute faith that whatever Bec did would be just brilliant.

Another time I sought Bec's advice was last year, when we organised the very first children's campout at Government House with the governor, and VicHealth Governor of Victoria, Patron-in-Chief Her Excellency The Honourable Linda Dessau AC. I spoke to the VicHealth team and they were aware of the scale and risk around the project and thought some additional support would be required. I was confident we could pull it off so I rang Bec and said 'Bec, come on, I reckon we can do this wild thing.' She agreed, we worked on it together along with the VicHealth team and created an awesome outcome for children who would never have access to such an opportunity.

To me, mentoring is about always being there for the other person, no matter what the circumstances. It is not that important to come from the same industry to be a good mentor. However, you must have a connection. You've got to be interested in them, you've got to want to support them, and you've got to be able to champion them. There are people that have asked me to be their mentors before, but it hasn't been the right fit for me. You need to go with your intuition around those decisions.

Recently I started supporting another ex-dancer from Stompin and I just joined her newly formed Board. It's another important relationship with an amazing artist who is forging a new path as a highly regarded independent choreographer. Helping that next generation, whatever role I might be in, is so fulfilling and such an important part of my life.

Bec's story

Kindred spirits

I remember meeting Jerril in Launceston and wanting nothing more than to be part of her life. As a sixteen-year-old, I remember thinking that we saw the world the same way. Following Jerril's example, I can visualise what kind of life I might be able to have. I watch the choices Jerril makes, and I think about where life might lead me if I make those choices, too. Meeting Jerril was like meeting a kindred spirit—a person who I could look up to, and someone to guide me through my professional and personal life.

Our mentoring relationship was born out of a creative space, but it was also a friendship. Jerril always said to me, 'Don't worry, I'll always have your back'—on both a personal and professional level. That has been the gold nugget in our relationship, and has given me so much confidence, and sense of personal agency in everything I do.

What would Jerril do?

When I've got a big professional—or personal—decision to make, my modus operandi is to take a breather and think, 'What would Jerril do?' For instance, one of the things Jerril excels at is translating artistic language for people who don't have an artistic background. So when I'm at a daunting middle management board meeting full of people who don't come from the artistic world, I think about the kind of language Jerril would use and how she would help people to shift their perspectives.

I've got your back

I felt a huge sense of responsibility when Jerril handed Stompin over to Luke and I. It was a baptism of fire. As twenty-two-year-olds, we were at the beginning of understanding how to lead a dance company or communicate with a board. We leaned heavily on Jerril's mentorship for the first couple of years, learning what governance was all about, and how to lead the organisation as both artistic creators in the studio and leading the company from the frontline. I was so green when I started, I remember asking Jerril 'What's an excel spreadsheet?' For the first year, I felt like I was on the phone to Jerril almost every week.

She stayed with us at some really key points throughout that first year of transition, but still empowered us to lead. She was holding our hands in the gentlest and most practical way but at the same time letting us go, with the message 'Alright guys, it's your work now, make the things you want to make'. She placed an extraordinary level of trust in us.

The first funding application Luke and I wrote was for a triennial to the Australia Council. Jerril was heavily involved in all the drafts, asking us tough questions to ensure we found the correct wording. We knew the enormous benefits of a dance program like Stompin—how it transformed the lives of young people in Launceston—but we needed to communicate our vision succinctly to others who had no direct experience with the dance company. I remember ringing her in a time of doubt, and she said 'Bec, this will not fail'. It was at that moment that it hit me: 'Okay, it can't fail because we know Jerril has our back.'

By the second year we were starting to find our feet. After the second major show, Jerril said to us: 'You guys are sweet now, call me when you need me.'

Growing out of my mentor's shadow

About a year after we had been in the artistic directorship roles, we started feeling more confident, and there was more space between our meetings with Jerril. I had promised myself that I would do what I could for other young people, in my own confident and authentic way.

> *I believe I have a responsibility to other young people—that I can offer them something that might totally shift their lives, the way Jerril had shifted mine.*

In my third year at Stompin, a long term personal relationship ended and it forced me to reflect on where I was going with my life. I had a yearning to find my own sense of internal peace and needed the courage to realise it. So I decided the time was right to make a break, not just from the personal relationship but more broadly, from Launceston and Stompin. I remember calling Jerril with some trepidation and in tears. Her immediate response was to reassure me, and to talk through managing the transition in a pragmatic way. She took away all my fear. It didn't feel like such a terrifying move anymore. Jerril just guided me through the process of letting go. It was a great thing to me as a mentee, to know that she wasn't going to judge me or my decision.

Never far away

After I left Stompin I was freelancing for a time, living in Perth and travelling around Australia, but Jerril and I still kept in touch. She was the artistic director at Footscray Community Arts Centre—and she did a sneaky, wonderful thing where she said, 'Just come over for a chat'. I thought I'd be looking at a venue for a show that I was producing, but instead she told me 'I think you'd better work here'. I was really excited to be finally working with Jerril again. She was again responsible for the next huge professional chapter in my life. I had only known her through Stompin, and I was really thrilled to be learning from her in this very different context. By bringing me over, Jerril gave me scope to grow beyond dance and apply what I had learned through Stompin across diverse art forms. I was truly on board with her artistic vision for the community, and just loved observing her with a different team, leading in a very different way. It was fascinating to see how she applied the principles from her artistic background to create an artistic vision and bring others along who don't come from an arts background.

That move, nearly ten years ago, started my love affair with the western part of Melbourne and the artists there. I've been deeply connected to the west ever since.

Applying life's learnings

Jerril showed me that I could create an artistic life, but for it to have any currency to me it needs to have a place in the community. That's what Jerril showed me right from the beginning. She taught me how to be in the world and that is a wonderful and rare thing.

Some of the mentoring relationships I have with young and emerging artists today are formal, some informal. The greatest lesson I've learned from Jerril is her mantra 'Don't worry, I've got your back'. I apply it to all my mentoring relationships. I make time for each mentee to really listen, let them stumble, and to let them work it out in their own time if they need to. I just reassure them that I have their back.

As the mentorship with Jerril has grown, I've looked forward to being able to give back to her in ways the sixteen-year-old me couldn't have possibly imagined.

1 www.stompin.net

Reflections

For mentors

- What does 'I've got your back' mean in the context of your mentee relationship?
- As a role model for younger women how do you mentor them in a way where they learn from you but don't become a clone of you? How can you empower them to become their own person and take their own path in life?
- How do you help your mentee move from being dependent on your guidance to thinking independently?
- Where might there be opportunities for you to be mentored by a younger person to provide a different perspective to your decision-making? What might you learn from the experience?

For mentees

- Can your immediate boss also be your mentor? How might that work?
- Can you think of circumstances where you may have benefited from asking 'what would my mentor do or say?' Are there situations coming up in the near future where this approach would be helpful?
- What self-limiting beliefs do you hold about yourself? When did they emerge? What strategies can you identify to eliminate or neutralise these beliefs?
- What do you feel unprepared for or unqualified to take on right now? What might help you overcome this?

Mentoring matters

◇◇◇◇◇

Anita Curnow
& Sophie Atkinson
VicRoads

Anita Curnow

Since graduating as an engineer in the 1990s, Anita has dedicated her career to a safe, reliable and sustainable transport system. She joined VicRoads in 2003 as Manager, Road Based Public Transport. Fifteen years on, she is one of VicRoads' Executive Directors. As one of the few executive women engineers at VicRoads, Anita has been instrumental in raising awareness of the obstacles women engineers face, and in leading the drive to create greater opportunities for technical women to excel in their careers.

Sophie Atkinson

Sophie joined VicRoads as a graduate engineer. After returning from the UK with a Master's degree, she sought out Anita to help her apply her passion for creating a sustainable transport system. When Sophie embarked on the first structured mentoring program offered at VicRoads, their bond became even stronger.

Anita's story

A meeting of minds

I first met Sophie back in 2012. She was completely committed to implementing a socially and environmentally sustainable transport system in Australia, but was finding herself somewhat lost in navigating VicRoads. I had a similar passion for sustainable transport and was determined to help her succeed, so an informal mentoring relationship began. I remember the fantastic support provided by my General Manager when I first arrived, and how valuable it was to have some guidance navigating the internal structures and decision-making processes. I wanted to give the same kind of support to Sophie. Although my journey was different, my experiences and story may help her navigate some of her own challenges.

A tough initiation

My own journey into VicRoads began when I was working at the Department of Infrastructure. I was feeling somewhat stuck in my role, and so I started looking beyond the Department for a career move. One day I opened up the newspaper and saw my perfect job advertised—Manager of Road Based Public Transport at VicRoads. It had my name all over it, so I just had to apply. I was thrilled when I was successful.

From day one, I quickly came to realise that the organisation could be somewhat of a battleground—one for which I wasn't fully prepared. There had been along held culture of strong criticism from the top, and I remember feeling quite frightened that I would say something wrong or look silly when I had to present to the corporate management group.

Things are changing now, but back then there were pockets within VicRoads that operated like a boys' club. It was very hard to get traction as a woman—to progress or to even feel that people would accept my contribution. This was difficult for me, because I really needed to feel that I was contributing and making a difference. I didn't really understand the reason for the resistance, and felt somewhat ill-equipped to tackle it. I eventually learned that earning the respect of people in the regions, and getting them on board with what I was trying to achieve, was critical to achieving change. It was a tough learning curve.

The formal mentoring program at VicRoads has been enormously successful since its introduction in 2014. I was one of the founding mentors of the program, and this is when I began to formally mentor Sophie. The program included frameworks for discussion, a weekly video tape for review, regular scheduled meetings and peer group meetings with women sharing their experiences. It was originally structured around weekly catch-ups, but that became unrealistic with current workloads and required homework between sessions, so it would often stretch out to fortnightly meetings. The program structure has changed accordingly, and is now based around fortnightly sessions, over a six-month period, which is a better timeframe.

The formal program provided Sophie with a context and framework, almost like a launching pad for a conversation. The timing was perfect, as Sophie had just been appointed to an acting people leader role. This meant she could directly apply the concepts we discussed in the mentoring program to her real-life situation. I could see her climbing this enormous learning curve, and absorbing everything in the program because of its direct relevance to her day to day leadership challenges.

Inspiring leaders and role models

When I first joined VicRoads, Ted Vincent, my General Manager was a great support and inspiration. Ted taught me how to navigate the world of VicRoads—how decisions are made, how to engage my team and internal stakeholders. He also taught me to answer my own questions. Although not a formal mentor, Ted encouraged me and was a great supporter when I needed one.

Then there was Janet Brash, who also reported to Ted. I thought Janet was fantastic. She was a bit older than me, a bit more experienced and had been an executive for a bit longer. She was an engineer as well. She was a bit of a trailblazer, and I really loved working with her. I aspired to be like her. I just loved the way she was respected for her technical knowledge and how she collaborated with others. I still reflect on Janet's journey from time to time, and on the courage she showed at VicRoads.

Accelerating change

Ten years into my career at VicRoads there were still only six women amongst the seventy or so executives, and just two of us were engineers. I knew there were all these female engineers out there but I didn't see them progressing into executive roles.

I wanted to understand what was stopping women getting to the top, so I led the development of a survey to identify the issues that were affecting their retention and overall quality of life.[1] One clear message was that, while many women felt part-time and flexible arrangements were readily available, they found their careers suddenly stalling once they accessed these policies. Promotions dried up, and they wereautomatically excluded from consideration for management roles. The survey also uncovered a strong demand for formal and informal mentoring arrangements, and a need to provide broader networking opportunities amongst technical women.

Enter the diversity champion

Around the time these findings emerged, John Merritt was appointed as CEO to VicRoads. He had a reputation as a fierce champion of diversity and inclusion. With his personal commitment, a range of measures were put in place to eliminate barriers to career success and to creating a culture that embraced diversity and inclusion.

John's argument for diversity is compelling. 'VicRoads is a people business and people matter', he says.

> *At its heart, diversity, whether it is gender, race, culture, sexual preference, or disability, creates a culture that values difference and recognising that everyone matters.*

'Hearing the amazingly rich life stories of some of the women participating in the mentoring program, such as those from culturally and linguistically diverse backgrounds, leads us to consider how we can ensure these women, with their rich life stories, can contribute to VicRoads. People work for VicRoads to make a difference,' reflects

John, and diversity can help all of us make more of a difference in our workplace and in our community. The number of graduates from the MyMentor program who have since received a promotion is about forty-five percent. As more of these successful graduates representing diverse cultures continue to move up the managerial and corporate ladder it is inevitable that both VicRoads, and the broader community, will benefit from this combination of diversity and mentorship.

John was a great example of a leader walking the talk. I experienced this first-hand, initially being the only woman on the executive leadership team. At every meeting he'd ask me, 'What do you think about this, Anita?' I often hesitated, thinking 'I don't know.' When I provided a different perspective on an issue, he would point out to others just how important it was that I had made that contribution. It sometimes got to the point where I got tired of John asking me what I thought all the time. But upon reflection, I know what he was doing. He was building my confidence, and letting me know that my input was valued. That made me feel really good.

John not only informally mentored me, he actively advocated for me and provided me with an extraordinary opportunity to prove myself.I was incredulous when he invited me to act in the Executive Director Corporate Services role—it was a sideways move from one field to another, as well as an upward move. Even though I aspired to a more senior leadership role, I always imagined it would be in my technical area, not in a different part of the business. He told me, 'Go for it. Make it your own. Don't follow any rules that anyone else has set before you. It's your thing.' That was really empowering, and it taught me a lot about myself and my capabilities. I thoroughly enjoyed the six months spent in that role.

> *The formal mentoring program at VicRoads has been enormously successful since its*

introduction in 2013. The program aims to inspire, energise and motivate women to take charge of their careers, and create success in their lives.

It is now in its fourth year, and has directly touched the lives of over 100 female participants and had a ripple effect to many others, men and women, such as our culturally and linguistically diverse staff and others who have not had a strong voice. The program aims to give women a voice—a sense that they are operating in a workplace where they can thrive and flourish, and it aims to show they are valued by the organisation. The CEO's sponsorship has also been critical to its success. He attends all the launches and graduation ceremonies. Now it has grown to thirty participants per program, and each program is oversubscribed.

Over time,we have become more intentional about the women we accept into the program. We are specifically seeking women who feel they may be at a crossroads, or feel blocked; perhaps they have been applying for more senior roles and not getting them.We want women who are ready for something different but they haven't able to crack the nut. A lot of women from culturally and linguistically diverse backgrounds are also participating, so it's been a launching pad for broader diversity and inclusion outcomes that we hadn't anticipated when we first embarked on it.

The art and science of mentoring

I believe mentoring is both a science and an art. The science is implementing structured, formal mentoring frameworks applying techniques and methodologies embedded in the program. The art is about developing a mentoring capability that all leaders can apply every day. I have learned over the years that learning to ask the right questions, rather than relying solely on my own experience,is integral to the art of mentoring. If I don't jump in with my own solution straight away,I will see my mentees come up with better answers than I could have suggested. In this way, mentoring is a critical leadership capability. It teaches others to hone their critical thinking skills, to listen to their instincts and to use their judgement to make decisions that are right for them, rather than applying strategies that I might suggest based on my own experiences.

I encourage my mentees to be mindful of their feelings in different situations. If I can encourage them to be aware of what pushes their emotional triggers, they can develop mastery over how they will respond in future situations. With greater emotional awareness, we can develop deeper insights to look below the surface of a situation.

I now have mentoring relationships with a number of women, some through the formal program, others more informally. I also apply a mentoring mindset to my leadership style. I feel incredibly honoured when women share confidences with me, whether it is to talk through specific career challenges, or about how to manage their work-life balance. There have been times when I have been the first person at work they confide in when they are pregnant, and I help them through the process of advising their team and preparing for the next phase in their career.

Three steps forward

Whilst we have made great strides towards creating a truly diverse culture, we need to mature as an organisation. Embracing diversity and inclusion should become embedded in our DNA, and should not depend on the personal leadership and role modelling of our CEO and a small group of supporters. Whether John Merritt ends up being here for four years or ten, we have to get ourselves into a position where an inclusive collaboration becomes the fabric of the organisation. Long term, I will be looking for three signs that we have got there. First, that diversity initiatives are accessed by all employees, not just women. Secondly, that our workforce truly reflects the diverse community we serve. Finally, we become a place where people absolutely aspire to work.

Sophie's story

Finding my feet

I came straight to VicRoads from graduating with an Honours degree in engineering. I had completed several internships with other firms, but this was my first experience at VicRoads. I was accepted into the graduate program, which involved a series of rotations throughout VicRoads. Each rotation gave me great breadth of experience and a better understanding of the different parts of the organisation. It was also my first experience of being allocated a mentor.

At the end of the rotations, I was offered a permanent role in the surveying team. While I enjoyed working with this team, long term I felt the role was too technical. I wanted to do something strategic, and more aligned with my passion for sustainability so I decided to take a career break, and went to the UK to complete my Master's in Engineering for Sustainable Development at Cambridge University.

I returned to VicRoadsone year later, in 2012, eager to contribute and make a difference. I was keen to see my dreams and aspirations for sustainable transport systems come true. I consulted my mentor from the graduate program about how to achieve this, and he suggested I touch base with Anita, who was working in a similar area. Anita and I started having informal, general catch-ups about career aspirations.Through this relationship, I investigated taking on a secondment opportunity in the Network and AssetPlanning area.

Adding depth to the relationship

When we formalized the mentoring relationship through the MyMentor program in 2014, our bond grew to another level. The mentoring program gave us structure, content and a context for conversations beyond our ad hoc catch-ups. We were meeting more regularly and were thinking through themes and issues fairly systematically. Also, there was an accountability to get through all the modules because of the graduation at the end. We also got to know each other on a more personal level through this time, as we began sharing our life experiences.

Hearing Anita's stories and her perspective as we went along was really useful. It confirmed some of my experiences and thoughts, and I realised I wasn't alone in having to work through them.

The power of the program lay in its application to my day-to-day experiences. It is one thing to read an article or book that you agree with, whether it is about self-leadership or taking personal ownership. It is quite another to actually apply the theory in practice and then reflect on how it worked. I remember one part of the program about learning to speak up in meetings, which really resonated with me. On a few occasions, I had been fearful to speak up at meetings,so having some practical tools on hand that prepared me for the next opportunity was really powerful. Being able to go back to Anita and say, 'It worked!' was a great moment.

Conversations with Anita often moved beyond a specific topic in the program into broader applications. For instance, the module around learning to speak up at meetings morphed into a broader conversation about talking through difficult issues with staff. I was in my first acting role as a team leader, and had about twelve people reporting to me. I was having a variety of different conversations with team members, some of them pretty difficult. Anita had said, 'When you have a chat, take the time to reflect on it, and how you felt. What you actually said, what the person actually said and how that made you feel'. Often, I would leave a conversation feeling either frustrated or happy, not knowing what triggered any of these emotions. By documenting and reflecting on those conversations, I began to understand my emotional triggers and could prepare myself to respond more effectively in the future. Those conversations wereincredibly useful. You couldn't just pick that up from reading a book.

Work-life balance—you can't just set and forget

One of the great things I learned from the program was to develop a solid career path in the context of a broader life plan. People talk about work-life balance as if they are two discrete things, but really there are many facets to the intersection of work and life. There are career, relationships, health and well-being, finances, spiritual fulfillment, social and community involvement and fun and recreation. Thinking about life across all of these different segments was incredibly insightful, and helped me build a clear strategy for my life and my career. You've heard it all before, but taking the time to think it through, write it down and apply it to yourself is really powerful.

I also loved the personal branding exercise. Your personal brand is about clarifying your values, your life's purpose, your ultimate vision and what you want to be known for. It boils down to defining your unique attributes—your strengths, skills, values and passions that make you stand out. This exercise helped me think about how I want to be perceived by others, how I see myself and to plan how I'm going to share that with others.

We also established a peer mentoring group, which provided us with a support network of women also going through the program. We would meet regularly to share stories, discuss our thoughts and feelings, and raise any specific challenges or insights we had experienced at work and through the program. I felt this network provided yet another perspective and another source of advice.

For me, the power of the program lay in the support I received from Anita—listening to her

> *story, thinking about it, applying it to myself and having a group of women participating in the program going through it with me.*

It is about having someone like Anita there to flesh out what that means for me, where I'm going in the future.

Although the mentoring program formally ends after completing the twelve modules, it never really ends. I often apply what I've learned as my circumstances change, or when I need to make important decisions. I often think 'What would Anita do or say?' or 'If I had to explain it to Anita what would I say?' This is because Anita is so good at unpacking situations, looking below the surface and getting to the heart of the matter. I have also revisited work-life balance. Now that I'm a mother, for instance, I'm at a different phase in my life than when I first assessed all the components of my life and work. Back then, it was just my husband and I pursuing our careers, and we could work long hours fairly single-mindedly with a focus on advancing our own careers. Now that we are parents we need to factor another person in to our lives, and working through this structure at critical times helps me keep my life in perspective.

1 Women in Technical Roles in VicRoads, October 2013

Reflections

For mentors:

- What does the art and science of mentoring mean in your mentoring relationship? Is a formal, structured mentoring program initiated by your organisation more appropriate than a relationship that develops organically?
- When might it be appropriate to openly advocate for your mentee?
- How can you plan for the transitional process, when your formal mentoring relationship comes to an end?
- Should you make it clear that the relationship has come to an end when the formal process finishes, or are you prepared to keep the relationship going on an informal basis?

For mentees:

- How can you identify the best mentor for you at the right stage in your career?
- How can you approach a mentor and gain his or her agreement to mentor you?
- How can you get the most out of combining formal and informal mentoring? What issues would you raise and discuss in a formal program versus an informal one?
- Which elements of a formal mentoring program should you revisit periodically?
- What are the expectations, if any, between you and your mentor around keeping in touch after the formal relationship has ended?

Friends can be Mentors

◇◇◇◇◇

Kim Rubenstein & Larissa Halonkin
Australian National University (ANU)

Kim Rubenstein

Kim is a Professor in the Law School at the Australian National University. She was Director of the Centre for International and Public law from 2006 through until 2015. In addition, she was the inaugural Convenor (2011 – 2012) of the ANU Gender Institute. She is Australia's citizenship law expert and was one of the early instigators of feminist scholarly approaches to Australian constitutional law.

Larissa Halonkin

Larissa is a legal researcher. She first met Kim at university, with Kim teaching Larissa the compulsory law subject Constitutional and Administrative Law. Larissa later worked with Kim as her Research Assistant where a deep and special friendship blossomed, not only between the two women but also with their families.

The mentoring relationship in their professional capacities evolved and strengthened inextricably alongside the personal, and they cannot imagine how a successful mentor/mentee relationship could occur between them without an accompanying friendship. Trailblazing Women and the Law is their latest collaboration, an Australian Research Council funded project gathering oral histories to be added into the National Library of Australia's collection and to reflect on the experiences of women in the law and their 'active citizenship' in broader society.

Kim's Story

One of the real beauties of being an academic, that I find very nourishing, is that you meet individuals in your classrooms who stand out because of their interest in the subject and their approach. I think there's something unique about the teacher/student relationship that implicitly gives a teacher a mentoring role.

Getting started

Most of my mentoring has come from having a connection with a student whom I've got to know in the classroom context. We first met when Larissa was a student in my Constitutional and Administrative Law class. That was a yearlong subject, and I would see students twice a week for two hours each session. There was something about Larissa as a student that drew my attention, like when she would come up and ask questions after the class. This influenced my decision to chose Larissa when I had a particular research assistant role to be fulfilled. I felt she was the type of person I would like to work with, someone who was capable and trustworthy. I guess that's the time I made that transitional jump, from the teaching role to the mentoring role.

I don't think there is a formula for Larissa and me. I think it's slightly organic in the sense that it happens when it's needed. Larissa will initiate the relationship when she has questions. I don't have to think 'should I be contacting Larissa to see where she's at?' This is where we probably don't fit into any formal mentoring structure.

Friends make better mentors

We've become part of each other's lives, in a deep personal sense, yet I think this interview is really the first time I've considered friendship versus mentoring. How interesting that Larissa and I are collaborating on a project about the impact of women in law, and then discussing the impact of our own relationships on each other.

I would say we have similar personalities on some levels. We are both gregarious and at ease talking to other people. There are some more quiet students who would not have necessarily followed the track that Larissa's followed but with whom I've stayed in touch or they contact me for advice.

You can mentor women with very different personalities to you. But if we talk about deep

> *mentoring as opposed to formal mentoring you do need a sense of connection to the other person; you want to act in their best interests as a fellow human being, not just fulfill your professional responsibilities to a junior colleague, so that connection is essential.*

It's also interesting to reflect on the impact of gender and backgrounds on mentoring. I've mentored a few men who have been former students, but it's never been that sort of friendship that I have with the women I've guided. I stay in contact with them but I wouldn't meet them socially, and there are none of those men whose families have become family friends.

People's backgrounds are quite interesting too. I don't think it's essential to have the same cultural background or life experiences. People contact you by virtue of your expertise or the area in which you work, and their personal situation and needs. With Larissa our life experiences have been different. On the other hand, having some similarities can deepen and strengthen the relationship. For instance, I'm a white Jewish woman. Once I mentored an Iranian Muslim woman at the Australian National University (ANU). From a gender perspective I was conscious of her vulnerability and lack of knowledge. I connected with her even though she had a completely different background, but it was similar in its otherness—like me, she was not from a mainstream religion, and she was a woman.

The power of formal vs. informal mentoring arrangements

I think of formal mentoring in terms of having formal structures. There were no formal structures when I was a student at university. I would have had teachers that I spoke to, but that was self-initiated.

When I became an academic the people who mentored me were senior colleagues who I could approach to ask questions, but again, there wasn't a formal structure at that stage. The central Gender Equity Unit at the University of Melbourne later established a more formal mentoring framework and that is when I became a mentor to junior colleagues. Now, as a professor in the law school at ANU, I have junior colleagues allocated to me. I think being a supervisor is rolled into being a mentor in some way, because you're meant to be more than just the person signing off timesheets: you are there to guide them in their professional development and in their academic career.

This is part of the issue about mentoring; there's no clear delineation between the formal frameworks and the personal frameworks. That probably influences the way some people get more out of mentoring than others—those mentees who have the type of personalities where they easily interact with their mentors may maximise the opportunities provided by mentoring more than participants who don't have as organic a connection.

My approach to mentoring is to respond in an advisory way. I don't think I've ever thought of myself as coaching Larissa, because she's got her own capacity. I am her mentor because of the age difference, really. I started ahead of her, so I've got experience she can use.

Within the professional realm

In my experience I believe it is more valuable to be in the same professional realm as your mentee because you need to have a handle on the professional worlds in which you are mentoring—its language and its way of being. There's a structure and a way that you approach the world and operate that you probably don't really think about. At ANU a couple of my early mentees were from different disciplinary backgrounds. While I could give some advice in relation to the university structure, I didn't have the capacity to advise them on things that would be important to their specific discipline.

I see advocacy as different from mentoring. Advocacy is about acting on someone's behalf or progressing an agenda, an idea or an issue for them or contacting someone on their behalf. For instance, writing references for former students is a form of advocacy; it is not necessarily part of a mentoring relationship.

Networks become really important in mentoring, because you're not always able to give anyone the full complement of advice, but you can put people in touch with one another.

The PhD student who is funded by our ARC project we are both working on is looking at networks of association as an analytical tool, and how the women we are interviewing have different points of connection. You really need to analyse more than forty-five interviews to do a comprehensive analysis, but even within the forty-five you see how those forms of association are really important in people's lives. One of the research outputs is around understanding what women who didn't have those associations did with law, compared to women who were networked and well connected. Those who didn't have as many networks of association tended to be more strategic, or more thoughtful about using their law in a particular way because they needed to ask more questions to understand their environment, whereas women with stronger networked connections had a ready frame for navigating the system.

It's also been fascinating to see the impact of mentoring on women in each decade of the project. For example, pioneering female lawyers often found that men were willing to mentor them, or advocate for them. This might be for something as simple as organising barristers chambers to work from when they were otherwise denied access to office space. We also observed how some women established alliances with men from religious or cultural minorities—others who had an 'otherness' about them that allowed them to connect regardless of their gender.

Another interesting find was the way some women, particularly those with stronger connections, saw law as something that continues to govern society, not change it. Whereas those women who had fewer or weaker networks often saw law as a tool for social change.

Mentoring is about them, not you

As a mentor, the key is to be really open to the possibilities of how you can assist in someone else's life. This is about being open and listening to the person, understanding how you can help them and how your experience might be of benefit to them, without your input being the determinative answer for them.

Mentoring is not about you; it's really about the person you are mentoring. For example, when I became the Director of the Centre for International Public Law at ANU, I had a fantastic administrator. I could see she had so much more potential, and it seemed unfair for her to keep doing what she was doing, so I encouraged her to start a PhD. Even though it was not in my self-interest to lose her I knew that it was absolutely the right thing for her, and she's now doing other fantastic work.

When Larissa decided not to do a PhD (an option from the continuation of our project that arose as one of many for her) she was a bit worried about letting me down, but my response to her was along the lines: 'there are lots of people who can do a PhD, but it's got to be right for you, so you're not letting me down in any way. It's more about assessing an opportunity, but if it doesn't suit you it's really no skin off my nose.'

It's really interesting to reflect on what mentors get from a mentoring relationship. I get a sense of affirmation that what I'm doing in my role as an academic is important; that I'm able to inspire the next generation to go on and do things with their law degrees that are of benefit to society. Perhaps there is an egotistical aspect to it, as it does nourish me and it's nice to think I've had some sort of influence in another person's life. We bask in each other's glory and I'm so proud to be part of Larissa's life and her life choices. Also, the women I mentor are just really inspriational people, so my life is enhanced by relationships with people with whom I enjoy being around.

I've mentored men too, guiding them in their career choices, especially men who are interested in pursuing an academic career in the professional world in which I live. I can guide them and I open up my networks to them just as I would with my female mentees. However I have never developed that same depth of personal relationship with my male mentees. Somehow I don't get as much involved in their personal lives, or the lives of their families. Mentoring women somehow opens up opportunities for an intimate friendship that can be more tricky with men.

Larissa's Story

Kim and I first met in a classroom context. She taught a compulsory subject and I was at the very beginning of my law degree. I remember we talked about choice of subjects. When I was looking to do summer clerkships in Melbourne's law firms—and again when I was applying for articles—I asked her which direction to take in terms of subject matter or firm. I always knew that I could call on Kim to sound her out: 'I'm thinking about this position, what do you think?' So it's come full circle. We met all those years ago and still have kept in contact, which is most unusual.

Friend and mentor

In the early days of the mentoring relationship, I would initiate contact with Kim when I had a specific dilemma or issue I needed to explore. These days we have a more seamless kind of mentoring relationship, where we are always there for each other. It's a safe and comfortable place to be. Our relationship works in large part because of the mix of differences and similarities we bring to the relationship. We have had different life experiences and come from different family backgrounds, yet we have similar values, which is most important and common interests and purpose. We also have similar personalities, so we understand each other well. Perhaps that is the chemistry.

I guess we have a multifaceted friendship because Kim is a personal friend as well as a family friend. I invited Kim to my wedding and we've know each others' children since they were born. We visit as families and so it's even broader than just ourselves. But I absolutely see Kim as a mentor. There's a sense of clarity and wisdom in Kim that I draw upon.

When I think about mentoring, I don't see it in the clinical, professional sense, but across boundaries of friendship. There's nothing that's out of bounds; I could go to Kim to talk openly and honestly about anything.

Where friendship and mentorship could collide

Our mentoring relationship needs to be tempered by reality. Our relationship is unique because it is half random, half mentor. Sometimes they blend and you need to be careful. You don't want to take things for granted, or be inappropriate.

For example, I had an opportunity to complete a PhD with Kim where I could further explore the research data from our current project. That would have been of benefit to Kim, but ultimately I decided that it wasn't going to suit my personality and my circumstances. In that situation I felt that I was going to personally let Kim down as a friend. That's a really pertinent example of where the friendship and mentoring relationship can collide—you need to identify them and manage them appropriately.

Exploring options

I had been working part time at the Department of Justice for some time, but as good as the work was, I often felt I was treading water, I wasn't passionate about it and I felt myself becoming jaded. I realised the more substantial, higher level and intellectually challenging work could be available to me, but only if I was prepared to substantially increase my working hours, which was not what I wanted. Yet staying in my current role was not sustainable. In the back of my mind, I'd always considered a career in teaching. So I decided to explore this option further.

Kim was incredibly supportive and enthusiastic about the idea. Part of her generosity of spirit is about opening up her networks time and time again in all areas. Kim organised for me to meet with people she knew who also had a law degree and had chosen to explore teaching. After meeting with a number of people, and thinking about it further, I decided to take the plunge. I started the teaching degree and completed a placement before I realised that I missed the cut and thrust of legal work in the public sector, especially grappling with ideas and issues where you can see a real benefit to the community. I found teaching a bit restrictive with the bells going every forty minutes. I'd been very self- directed in my work previously so it was hard to begin a new area of work where I didn't have as much autonomy. I have no regrets that I explored teaching—it was good to get it out of my system and gave me a new-found respect and passion for working in government.

I don't know if this is a definition of mentoring, but there are times when I'm sure that Kim has acted against her own self-interest in exploring ideas or avenues for me. There's a respect and an openness, as well as a capacity to just listen; a willingness to engage with people, and wanting everyone to be at their best and to do their best.

Trailblazing Women in Law

The opportunity to work with Kim came at a time when I was considering taking a redundancy package from the Victorian government after ten years. I knew that I was walking away from wonderful working conditions. Although there were things that weren't ideal, there were many things that were, and I think Kim's project came at the right time. It enabled me to be available to take up Kim's Trailblazing Women in Law project and also to be around for my young daughters. So the timing was right for me.

Every woman's circumstance is different. The Male Champions of Change is a mentoring program where gender is actually really interesting. It's fascinating in that it's a formal mentoring proposal; using men who are already embedded in the system and who by their nature have open networks. It's a very positive thing, but part of me feels like somehow it's reinforcing the power of men—that women still need to rely on engaging powerful men to prioritise their issues, to endorse womenand to progress women's careers.

> *I would encourage anyone who's beginning his or her career to look for a mentor—someone who can guide them and simply act as an impartial sounding board.*

I think a mentor is a truly special kind of person in that regard, because there are too many other people in your life who might be self-interested, who may not understand the professional context in which you work, or may not have the wisdom you need. Having Kim is truly one of the luckiest aspects of my life, and I treasure it enormously. I think that every young woman, if they can develop that kind of relationship, would be really blessed.

Reflections

For mentors:

- Can a deep friendship develop successfully alongside a professional mentoring relationship?
- Are there circumstances where multiple roles of supervisor, mentor and friend could collide?
- Many mentoring relationships evolve into long term friendships. How do you maintain independence and boundaries when the relationship develops beyond the formal work based context?
- What benefits do you receive from the mentoring relationship?

For mentees:

- Do you feel you have the opportunity to work to your potential? If not, how satisfied are you with that situation right now?
- How important to you is similarity versus difference in cultural background or professional experience between you and your mentor? What could be the benefits and pitfalls of either scenario?
- Where are the boundaries in the mentoring relationship? Is there anything out of bounds that you do not want to discuss? If there are exclusions, why are you excluding these things?
- To what extent is work enabling you to realise your potential? What can you do about it?

Standing on the shoulders of giants

Advocacy and sponsorship —the critical element

'If I have seen further it is by standing on the shoulders of giants.'
— Isaac Newton.

The stories in this book indicate the critical role advocacy, or sponsorship, has played in accelerating the careers of women. While mentors can provide important emotional and career support, build self-confidence and provide wise career advice, sponsoring a mentee provides a deeper level of commitment. Mentors who are also advocates act on someone's behalf, or progress an agenda, an idea, or an issue for them. They are often key decision-makers in an organisation, such as a CEO or a senior executive with a voice when it comes to making appointments or influencing who receives promising opportunities and challenging assignments. They look after their mentees—they fight for them, promote their talents, encourage others to notice them, provide a voice for them at the decision-making table and protect them from unfair biases or perceptions. Whole careers have turned on relationships like these.

Mentoring and sponsorship—different but complementary interventions

Sponsorship differs from mentoring in several important ways. In a general sense, mentoring is more of a reflective, one-on-one confidential relationship between two people, whilst sponsorship looks outwards, and opens up the world to the mentee. Mentors provide one-on-one emotional support and feedback; they help their mentees navigate corporate politics they provide advice and share their own experiences. A sponsor, on the other hand, is usually a senior manager with influence providing their mentees with access to other executives who may influence their careers. They raise the visibility of their mentees, they fight for their mentees to get promoted and they may protect them from damaging contact with senior executives.

But does sponsorship really make a difference? Perhaps John Merritt, CEO of VicRoads described it best when he reflected on the enormous impact the formal mentoring program had on the lives of the participating women. On its third round now, and focusing on women from culturally diverse backgrounds this time around, the mentoring program has had a profound effect. The sheer experience of being with a group of women who are going through similar challenges at work—whether it be returning to work after having children, or dealing with assumptions about their gender or culture, is enormously powerful. To participate in the program and then feel affirmed by the organisation is also very moving and powerful, he observed. It takes courage for many of the women to participate on the program—they may have made many personal sacrifices for their family and their children up until now, and they have come to the point where they believe it's time to stand up and do something for themselves, in a manner that says 'I owe it to my children to be a role model.'

'Everyone needs a fan' says John. 'You need someone in your

corner pushing for you.' There is no more important time for mentors to sponsor women than during the performance review discussions held by senior managers. This is the time when, every six months, the leadership team review performance outcomes of the top 150 or so current and potential future executives and assess who is ready for a promotion, a challenging assignment or a secondment opportunity. Having a mentor in that room who can describe the mentee's capabilities and can advocate for her readiness is critical for raising the visibility of high performing women who historically have been unknown to the group or passed under the radar.

This type of mentor-sponsorship pays off. Around forty-five percent of mentees have been promoted, all of them on merit, as their talent has been recognised.

A growing body of global research also describes the central role advocacy can play in fostering talent and preparing women for senior roles.

The evidence

A global research study conducted in 2010 by Ibarra, Carter & Silva[1] followed the careers of over 4000 high potential men and women to understand the impact of mentoring on their careers. Their research indicated that the inclusion of advocacy in a mentoring relationship provided an enormous career advantage. However men were more likely to access sponsorship than women. Male mentors who mentored men, advocated for and actively sponsored their male mentees in a much more intentional and direct way then they did for their female mentees. This included introducing male mentees to key executives who could influence their next move, and actively sponsoring their male mentees for promotion—factors that were largely absent in women's mentoring experiences. Women in their study generally did not proactively engage in sponsor relationships when being mentored, and were less likely to build contacts than men. As a result, men receive a disproportionate career advantage to women when mentored, including fifteen percent more promotions and higher salaries than their female counterparts. The call to action from this study is for women to stand up and actively seek sponsorship from their mentors.

Sponsorship in Australia—do Australian women also miss out?

While the Australian research has not been as extensive as the global research to date, it does not necessarily support these conclusions. Kim Rubenstein and Larissa Halonkin have been studying the impact of mentoring on women in the legal profession in Australia for decades through their research project, *Trailblazing Women and the Law*[2], in which female lawyers and judges with careers that go back some seventy years were interviewed. Unlike the Ibarra *et al* study, Rubenstein and Halonkin concluded that women in Australia are indeed highly proactive in pursuing advocacy assistance, and experience it often. They were fascinated talking to pioneering female lawyers who had little trouble finding men willing to mentor or sponsor them, often for something as simple as organizing barristers' chambers to work from when they were otherwise denied access to office space. They also observed how some women established alliances with men from religious or cultural minorities. These men had an 'otherness' about them just as the women lawyers did, and this allowed them to connect and support each other, regardless of their gender. There are numerous other examples of successful sponsorship for these women lawyers. Here are just a few.

- A former partner of a commercial law firm speaks of the support she received from several male colleagues during her career. One introduced her to partners at his workplace, supporting her return to work and access to clients after maternity leave. Another was instrumental in referring work, enabling her to maintain a strong practice.

- An academic lawyer included in the study described having her name put forward for the role of deputy dean in a prestigious Australian law school, whilst another academic lawyer spoke of her recommendation for a position as a director of a legal centre.
- A highly-accomplished government and international lawyer spoke of a male colleague who was a strong advocate for women in senior positions, while a current member of the judiciary had her name put forward by a female colleague for a role as president of the Australian Law Reform Commission.
- A former member of the judiciary told of being asked whether she would be willing to have her name put forward for an appointment to the Supreme Court in an Australian jurisdiction
- One former member of the judiciary spoke of the advocacy she had received after her first legal aid trial. The presiding judge was so impressed that he made the effort to walk down to the Bar Association to tell the Registrar to give this female barrister more work.

Further evidence—Me and My Mentor

The experiences of the women in *Me and My Mentor* confirm the powerful interplay between mentoring and sponsorship for women in gaining recognition, becoming visible and having their voice heard. Although mentees spent time understanding their skills, their motivators and their development needs, many were also introduced to important networks and sponsored by their mentors for specific role or assignments. Each mentee described this combination of mentoring and sponsoship as pivotal to their personal and professional development, and to their subsequent career advancement.

Adam Fennessey describes his role as Kate's supporter and advocate, rather than mentor, because, as he says: 'she's already really good at what she does.' 'Advocacy was about me setting up an opportunity for success [for Kate]' says Fennessey. He believes a large part of mentoring is giving women encouragement, confirmation and confidence.

Kate would agree: 'Coming back from maternity leave into a new role and new team—the score was zero, and I needed to build up my scores, my credibility' she reflected. Having the advocacy and support from Adam was very important to her. If not for his encouragement and backing she believes she would not have accepted the key decision-making role he offered her and which projected her career into a new level of seniority.

Fennessey initially advocated for Kate not just because he wanted her to succeed, but also because he wanted his organisation to benefit from her talent and potential. He also began to see that gender diversity and flexibility was not just good for the organisation, but critical for its broader success with its community.

Jodi Fullarton-Healey went out of her way to advocate for her mentee, Sophie, as often as she could. 'When you've mentored someone for five, six years, you know them pretty well, so you're willing to share your networks and advocate on their behalf. Why wouldn't you?' she asks. Jodi's advocacy had a massive impact on Sophie's career, providing her with several internal job opportunities when her secondment ended. 'Jodi went above and beyond to make sure that the right thing happened, that I was considered for opportunities and that I was treated fairly,' recalls Sophie. For Jodi it seemed a natural thing to provide this level of support, encouragement and advocacy because it's something that she would have valued when she was in the early stages of her career.

Carol Pollock says her PhD supervisor and mentor, Michael Field, actively supported her at a critical juncture in her career. She had applied for a promotion to a professor positionat only thirty-nine years of age and everybody said she was too young. Michael presented her case to the academic committee, urging them to consider her ability to meet the selection criteria and to not exclude her because of her age. She is sure his support helped her secure the professorship.

Sarah Glastras, one of Carol's mentees, says that despite not knowing her well Carol became her biggest advocate and wrote amazing references for her scholarship application for a prestigious NHMRC scholarship, which she was fortunate to secure.

John Merritt informally mentored Anita Curnow, but also actively advocated for her and provided her with an extraordinary opportunity to prove herself. 'I was incredulous when he invited me to act in the Executive Director Corporate Services role,' Anita said. 'It was a sideways move from one field to another, as well as an upward move. Even though I aspired to a more senior leadership role, I always imagined it would be in my technical area, not in a different part of the business. He told me "Make it your own. Don't follow any rules that anyone else has set before you. It's your thing." That was really empowering, and it taught me a lot about myself and my capabilities.' In a lovely example of three-generational mentoring within a single organisation, Anita now mentors colleagues more junior to her, but describes herself as a real fan of her mentee, Sophie: 'I drop her name quite often for things that could be done, or need to be done, opportunities that come up, however informal.'

Cindy Briscoe had to take deliberate steps to get noticed once she decided to step out of her specialist role. She did this by applying for a job 'out of left field', that would expand her horizons and demonstrate her interest and desire to step up and out. Although she wasn't selected for that role, making herself noticed was still worthwhile: one of the Commissioners recognised the broader contribution she could make, and became her advocate, sponsoring her when other opportunities arose.

Turning sparks into flames

'You've got to open doors for other women because often they won't open them for themselves. When you're on a selection panel, if there aren't enough women in the field, go out and encourage some.'
— Michaelia Cash, Minister for Women

Many of the mentors interviewed in *Me and My Mentor* described a personal mission to help younger women succeed. For Cindy Briscoe mentoring and advocacy is her passion, something she believes in strongly. 'Women like me have a special role as advocates for other women to ensure they are being considered for broader opportunities' she says. 'There are few senior women leaders in the Australian Public Service, even less who are truly passionate about making a difference.'

Advocacy—a necessary but not sufficient strategy

Despite the many positive experiences of women such as those profiled in this book women working across all professions and sectors continue to struggle for recognition and promotion to senior careers. The most recent senior executive consensus, conducted by Chief Executive Women (CEW) in 2017, found that women hold just twenty-one percent of senior executive positions, and forty of the top 200 companies in the AX200 have no females on their senior executive teams.[3]

Sponsorship is a significant strategy for women however it is important not to become over-reliant on it, or on the mentoring relationship as a sole strategy for success. Mentors may provide strong support, but it is not an effective stand-alone strategy to overcome other obstacles women exclusively experience and which continue to advantage men.

First, and perhaps the most significant barrier women face in reaching the top, is the effect of unconscious bias caused by ingrained beliefs about men's superior capability over women. This affects the selection process when choosing for significant or powerful operational roles, leaders of large business units, and for other experiences and roles considered essential for future CEOs. The CEW research found that 126 companies, or almost two thirds of the ASX200 companies, have no females in the key positions that are responsible for large commercial outcomes, and that command the highest salaries. This includes roles such as chief executive, chief operating officer or group executive positions. Women are more likely to be found holding support or functional roles, such as human resources (seventy-five percent of these roles are held by women), or corporate affairs (fifty-two percent).[4] The dominance of men in these senior leadership roles is reinforced by the unconscious power that prevailing conditions have on people's expectations and choices, and a tendency for many to recruit 'people like us'. Women are often simply not considered for positions that have been traditionally held by men, so they remain pigeon-holed in support roles. Without being considered of course, the problem is only exacerbated so that women miss out, not only on the higher paying roles, but for the opportunity of new experiences, career development and ultimately, access to key leadership positions.

Secondly, decision-makers also often make grossly inaccurate generalisations and assumptions about the availability of women for senior roles. The most pervasive assumption is that once women start a family they are no longer available to travel or take on challenging roles involving long hours. Consequently, women continue to be excluded from many senior level roles after becoming a parent—a disadvantage that men just don't experience.

Thirdly, childcare must become more available and more affordable. Limited access to childcare and the current tax and transfer system financially disadvantages mothers re-entering the workforce.[5]

Finally, many women are not natural self-advocates and will

often hold themselves in check with persistent self-doubts about their capability. No matter our skills, capabilities and brilliance, this lack of self-confidence can be a real career blocker for women. If women only apply for roles when they feel one-hundred percent capable, they miss out on a range of growth opportunities for which their male counterparts with less experience, would gladly put up their hand.

Jobs for the girls? Is there a downside to advocacy?

In big organisations, one of the risks of sponsorship is that it can be perceived as patronage—that a woman was appointed not on merit, but because of her mentor or sponsor's influence. This perception is a particular challenge in organisations that have gender equity targets, where women may be the focus of judgments such as 'she only got the job because she is female', or because the team needed to meet its gender targets.

How do we overcome this perception and ensure women are recognised on their merits? The mentors interviewed in this book are very clear about drawing a line in the sand—performance is the bottom line and appointments should be based on an individual's capabilities to do the job. Adam Fennessey put it this way: 'In my rhetoric, and I hope in my action, I always pull it back to capability.' Cindy Briscoe put her mentee in touch with other people in her department who were looking for her mentee's skill set, and then stepped aside. By simply introducing people to each other, she explains, you are not doing anything that might be seen as nepotism, but are merely facilitating contact and letting them take it from there.

Whilst this is true, women sometimes wonder at the double standards that can apply; where men seem to get the job often because of who they know, whereas women have to jump over extra hurdles to meet strict selection criteria and demonstrate that they deserve the job again and again before being accepted as legitimately holding office.

Be seen, be safe—strategies for success

Sophie Wilson reflects that one of the best pieces of advice she ever received from her mentor, Jodi was to advocate for herself. 'You need to ensure you are noticed. It's not enough to be a hard worker, there are lots of hard workers here,' Jodi reminded her.

Women need to have the courage to advocate for themselves, Sophie believes. Her advice to mentees is to identify people outside their immediate reporting sphere, who could sponsor them, advocate for them and advance their career. Then think about how you can demonstrate to them who you are and how you can show your capability.

Perhaps the most important strategy for women is to target organisations that are good for their career advancement. In these organisations women are highly visible, holding senior roles that include line management and commercially focused roles. These types of organisations are inevitably headed by a CEO who recognises the business imperative to attract, develop and promote women, and who creates a culture that seeks and respects diversity and holds managers accountable for delivering on diversity targets. Heather Carmody, Principal at the Nous Group, expressed it succinctly in *Sideways to the Top*: 'If the CEO is not noisy about the subject in an authentic way then it may be time to pack your bag of tricks and try elsewhere.'[6]

High visibility is critical for women. Evidence shows that the strongest predictor of success in women's advancement is the number of women working in that area.[7] It makes sense. As women become more visible and more women succeed in non-traditional, senior decision-making roles their presence will become less remarkable, stereotypes will change and there will be a greater willingness to hire more.

Mentoring relationships are critical for providing such visibility, and can play a central role in fostering talent and preparing women for senior positions. When combined with a strategic approach to selecting a supportive organisation, and acquiring broad based experience across a range of critical roles, mentoring and advocacy can be a powerful combination to turbo-charge careers.

1 Ibarra, H, Carter, NM & Silva, C 2010, 'Why men still get more promotions than women', Harvard Business Review, vol. September, pp. 80-85.

2 www.tbwl.esrc.unimelb.edu.au

3 Reported in The Australian, 8 September, 2017, p. 19

4 Ibid

5 For a more complete discussion of these issues go to www.kellyodwyer.com.au/matter-of-public-importance-the-importance-of-childcare/.

6 Sideways to The Top – 10 Stories of Successful Women That Will Change Your Thinking About Careers Forever, N. Breekveldt, Melbourne Books, 2013, p. 224.

7 Ibid

Conclusions

Mentoring—a concept whose time has come

'An enemy will agree, but a friend will argue.'
— Russian proverb

Although this book is limited to a small sample of eleven mentoring relationships it confirms much that has been said and written about the benefits of good quality mentoring for women's careers. Mentors play a crucial role for women in the workplace. In male-dominated workplaces, mentors—whether male or female—can level the playing field for women and lift barriers to career advancement, helping them identify strategies for overcoming inherent biases and stereotypes that continue to hold women back. High visibility and exposure to senior leaders is critical for women.

By sharing their own experiences mentors can inspire, provide guidance and help mentees explore options when faced with challenges or dilemmas. Ultimately, great mentors and great mentees set in train a dynamic and hugely beneficial process not just for themselves but for all their workplace and professional colleagues.

Re-imagining mentoring

Many formal corporate mentoring programs are established around the conventional, top down structure, where a senior decision-maker or 'elder' is allocated to a more junior high-potential individual. They usually meet at regular intervals, follow a prescribed process,often with a structured program of activities, and work together for a fixed period of time. These programs can be a rewarding, empowering and invaluable experience for younger talent in navigating the world of work. However workplace mentoring these days goes beyond this formal, hierarchical approach and can be powerful and transformational for both mentor and mentee. Take, for instance, the mentoring relationship between Jerril Rechter, CEO of VicHealth, and Bec Reid, dancer, now also producer, director, choreographer and artistic director. These days Jerril seeks out Bec's guidance and counselfor a reality check, in a way that reverses the original mentoring relationship that commenced a decade before. Adam Fennessey, formerly with the Victorian Department of Environment, Land, Water and Planning (DELWP), also regularly seeks out the views and advice of his mentee, Kate. Cindy Briscoe, Deputy Secretary of the Federal Department of Agriculture and Water, described how, as Tina Chawner's mentor, she was able to reflect on the way her own working life panned out and better understand the decisions she made along the way.

The reality for mentees is that mentoring is an evolving process, often with shifting boundaries and changing landscapes. Mentoring does not always follow a clear set of guidelines, or obey an orderly theoretical definition. Despite cautionary advice in many 'how to' books about separating mentoring from other relationships such as coaching and advocacy, the reality of mentoring is that it is often a messy process that can zig-zag in and out of these boundaries. In reality, mentoring is multi-dimensional. It can follow a conventional top down mentoring approach, yet could also involve peer-to-peer mentoring or reverse mentoring, with the younger mentor providing fresh insights or reality-checks to an older mentee. Some mentors counsel and directly advise their mentees, others use a more indirect coaching approach, adopting an inquiring, questioning style to assist their mentee discover their own path forward. Some relationships are for a fixed period, others are open-ended and may last a lifetime. Many mentors cross the professional divide and become firm friends with their mentees without compromising the integrity of the mentoring relationship.

Establishing an effective mentoring relationship

The stories in this book illustrate many good practices that excellent mentors consistently adopt to create a positive mentoring relationship, and that mentees adopt to maximise the benefits from the relationship.

The starting point for any successful relationship is clarity of purpose, objectives and boundaries. Great mentors ensure expectations and boundaries are clarified at the outset so that the mentee's expectations match what the mentor is prepared and able to provide. Useful questions to ask at the commencement of a mentoring relationship are:

- Will the relationship be based on an informal or formal relationship, will it be an ongoing partnership or a fixed period of support?
- Is the relationship based on sharing advice, technical knowledge and experiences, or on providing emotional support, or a combination of both?
- Will a similar background and industry experience be useful, or would it be more helpful to be mentored by someone from a different background and with a different perspective?
- Is networking important and is the mentor prepared to share his or her networks?
- Does the relationship include actively advocating and fighting for the mentee's advancement, or will it be based on providing a confidential and discrete sounding board and process of reflection?

- What style works best and is the best fit for the situation—telling, asking, encouraging, pushing boundaries or providing reassurance? It could be several of these, and they may change over time as the mentee develops in their professional life.

The answers to these questions will be dependent on the needs of the mentee and their career stage. Mentors and mentees who have these conversations early in the relationship will set up the relationship for success and reap the rewards.

Beyond this starting point, what does good mentoring look like, and how does a mentee know if they are being mentored well?

The driving forces behind successful mentors

There are many characteristics of great mentors. Yet out of the relationships chronicled in *Me and My Mentor* six traits consistently emerged, which mentors identified as critical success factors and which mentees attribute to accelerating their career success. If you are a mentee seeking a mentor, investigate the potential mentor for the following qualities.

1. **Commitment.** The mentor is fully committed to the relationship, being available whenever possible, when the mentee needs her or him, and openly sharing lessons from their own career journeys including their stumbles as well as their successes. The very best mentors are always available for a talk, and stick with their mentees through togh times. Great mentors don't just have an open door approach, they take the door off the hinges!
2. **Challenge.** Great mentors challenge mentees. Mentors are fully invested in the success of their mentees, acting as honest critics, pushing and challenging their mentees and providing critical feedback and encouragement they may not receive

from others. These mentors recognise when they need to steer the mentee in a specific direction, but also when to step back andencourage their mentee to arrive at their own conclusions and think through problems independently.

3. **Empathy.** The mentor possesses a genuine concern for the mentee coupled with a non-judgmental approach. This combination of factors enable mentees to feel safe to openly and confidentially discuss their needs and circumstances, disclosing weaknesses and self-doubts and developing the courage to experiment knowing their mentoring relationship provides a safety net.
4. **Reciprocal.** Positive mentoring is built on a foundation of equality, where the relationship is reciprocal and enriching for both the mentor and mentee. Even where a mentor may be the more senior person, they are open to learning from their mentee, using the relationship to reflect on her own learning and development, and the insights and knowledge her mentee provided.
5. **Knowing thyself.** An outstanding mentor will challenge their mentee to identify what they stand for—their own internal motivators and values, their passions and their drivers. They help mentees become mindful of their feelings, understand what pushes their buttons, and to develop and trust their intuition. They encourage the mentee to apply this insight to help find inner meaning and purpose, and authentically address situations, issues and decisions facing them. A great mentor is also aware of her own strengths, weaknesses, personality, and what drives her, and uses this self-insight to maximise the mentoring relationship.
6. **A mentoring mindset.** Excellent mentors have a reputation for applying a mentoring mindset to all interactions at work, with direct reports, peers or even upward mentoring to more

senior leaders. It's a way of leading and engaging with others, not just a skill that is dusted off and exercised exclusively in a mentee relationship.

The driving forces behind successful mentees

Just as mentors demonstrated consistent traits, the mentees who made the most of the mentoring relationship generally drew on a common set of attributes too. If you are a mentor who has been approached by a potential mentee, seek out these traits in them.

1. **They are proactive.** Great mentees put themselves out there and actively seek out mentoring relationships. They may meet someone at a work event, connect through a friendship or through another person's network. Whichever way, they will identify someone with a like-minded approach to the world, and take the initiative to seek out a mentoring relationship with them.
2. **They take responsibility.** The best mentees clearly communicate the things they need and would like from the relationship. They are clear about their needs from the relationship, take charge of meeting times, and come prepared with specific issues or dilemmas to discuss, always being respectful of their mentor's time.
3. **They are prepared to make themselves vulnerable.** Great mentees are prepared to openly discuss their fears, vulnerabilities and shortcomings. They are open about their mistakes. They seek out and appreciating tough feedback, and take action where needed. Great mentees aren't afraid to experiment with courageous action and make bold career choices, confident that the mentor 'has their back'.
4. **They listen and reflect.** Great mentees reflect on the advice they receive from their mentors, how it has been helpful, how they have adapted their style and decisions, and how

they have grown personally and professionally as a result of the mentoring experience.

5. **They adopt a mentoring mindset.** Great mentees build a circle of mentors—cultivating a network of influential peoplewho meet their varying needs at different career stages.They listen to the voices of these mentors to gain perspective and make informed choices. They often reflect on 'what would my mentor do?'
6. **They give back.** Great mentees are driven to become mentors themselves, passing on the gifts and benefits they received to others, so that a mentoring community is formed and becomes self-perpetuating.

The art and science of mentoring

Mentoring is an ever-changing mix of both art and science. Formal mentoring programs are the science—they provide a solid foundation of mentoring theory and methodologies, using a step-by-step systematic approach, accompanied by practical exercises and bounded by a specific timeframe to ensure clear objectives are met. They also provide an employer-sanctioned engagement with a leader or key decision-maker and signal to women that their career development is important. Formal mentoring programs like the My Mentor program[1] between Anita Curnow and Sophie Atkinson (chapter 10), Lynn Corcoran and Delphine Merino (chapter 3) and Cindy Briscoe and Tina Chawner (chapter 7) demonstrate the science of mentoring in action.

Informal mentoring is about the art—it is not reliant on sequential activities or control, but recognises the complexity and creativity required to work through mentoring challenges. Informal mentoring often begins with a casual encounter over a coffee or lunch, which tends to evolve into a more regular arrangement. Informal mentoring can also be based on making the most ofcasual mentoring opportunities at every opportunity. Many of the mentoring relationships in *Me and My Mentor* began from informal relationships that evolved organically. Sophie Wilson fortuitously sat next to Jodi Fullarton-Healy at a business lunch (chapter 5); Bec Reid identified a kindred spirit in Jerril Rechter and just wanted her to be part of her life (chapter 9). In many cases a friendship grew, like the relationship between Kim Rubenstein and Larissa Halokin (chapter 2) and between Adam Fennessesy and Kate Houghton (chapter 4). The mentee usually did not ask 'will you be my mentor?' in these situations.When the opportunity arose, however, the mentoring relationship strengthened and became flexible based on situations and needs, often over an extended period. Many formal mentorships also developed into informal relationships after the formal program concluded.

The science and art of coaching is like the yin and yang. Formal and informal, structured and emergent, time bound and timeless, these opposite forces can actually be complementary, so that when the art integrates with the science, the best results are produced.

Conclusions

Whilst there are many strategies women adopt to create career success, mentoring relationships can play a central role in fostering talent and preparing women for senior positions. Women who are well connected and who are on the talent radar of key decision-makers are more likely to be considered for that plum assignment, the next promotion or an interesting sideways move, than women who remain quiet achievers and hope their talents and track record will speak for themselves.

There are many faces to mentoring, there is no definitive right way to mentor, and no one-size-fits-all approach.This flexible approach is often the secret to its success, as the relationship evolves to meet the mentee's emerging needs and different circumstances. Structure is important and clarifying expectations at the commencement of the mentoring relationship is critical. Then, if the relationship is allowed to evolve naturally, the magic of mentoring happens.

Mentoring sets in train a dynamic and hugely beneficial process not just for the mentee, but for the entire workplace. Gender diverse leadership improves the bottom line of business. Mentoring programs attract and retain successful women and inspire them to be their best and reach their potential. A mentoring mindset is a critical leadership capability that, when applied, transforms individuals and teams. The contribution of everyone in the workplace is enhanced when leaders adopt a mentoring mindset through empathy, listening, engaging, influencing, inspiring, and fostering collaboration. When all these factors work in synchronicity, the potential of everyone in the business is realized to its fullest extent. Who wouldn't want to invest in mentoring?

1 *My Mentor Courageous Women*, by Maureen Frank, Emberin, 2014

Acknowledgements

I am immensely grateful to a number of individuals for helping to bring this book to life.

At the top of the list is Associate Justice Mary-Jane Ierodiaconou. She is one of the greatest advocates of women I know, and has transformed the lives of countless women in her orbit. This book would not have come about without her encouragement. She sparked my interest in writing about the impact of mentoring in women's careers after she referred me to a recent National Attrition and Re-engagement Study (NARS) of women in the legal profession. The study found that close to one in three women lawyers felt their career progression failed to live up to their expectations, in sharp contrast with less than one in five lawyers who were men. It also revealed that a well-designed mentoring program was a key strategy to support their career success.[1]

This was a challenge I found irresistible, and so my quest began: collecting stories of mentoring experiences from women across a wide range of ages, professions, sectors and geographies as the basis for understanding what successful mentoring was all about.

This leads me to offer a huge thank you to my community of professional colleagues, for opening doors and introducing me to the exceptional women profiled in this book. I am also grateful for their conversations as the book began to take shape. They challenged me to think deeply and sometimes in different ways about the themes and concepts that arose.

A tremendous thank you goes to the women featured in this book—mentors and mentees alike. The eleven mentees frankly and courageously shared their anecdotes of working through uncertainty, taking risks, leaping into the unknown and crashing through barriers. Their mentors generously shared their wisdom, reflections and practical insights with me and they have deepened my understanding of what it means to be able to truly live your passion at work. In every case their relationships developed way beyond a formal mentoring connection into a deep, lasting and life-changing friendship. It was a real joy to be part of these women's lives for the short period of writing this book.

To Carissa Goudey and to Emma Russell from History@Work who graciously played the role of external editor. Her calm and patient way of posing questions and providing countless suggestions helped shape the flow of the book and her contribution was indispensable in bringing the vision of this book to life.

I am deeply grateful to David Tenenbaum and the wonderful team at Melbourne Books, for supporting my love of writing, and designing and producing an outstanding product.

Finally, I thank my husband Andrew for being my best friend and partner in life. I am constantly amazed at his never-failing love, encouragement and unending patience as I disappear into my office for yet another period of hibernation only to emerge somewhat dazed several hours later. I couldn't imagine being on this book journey with a stronger advocate and supporter.

1 www.lawcouncil.asn.au/lawcouncil/images/LCA-PDF/Media-News/NARS_FactSheet_Complete_FINAL.pdf

Sideways To The Top 10 Stories Of Successful Women That Will Change Your Thinking About Careers Forever Norah Breekveldt

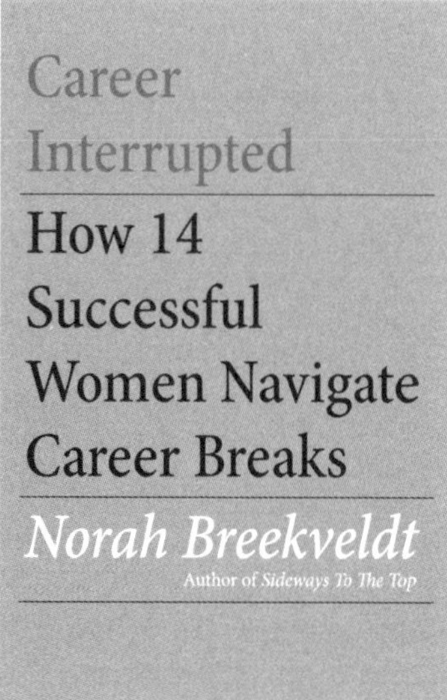

Also by Norah Breekveldt

- *Sideways To The Top: 10 Stories of Successful Women That Will Change Your Thinking About Careers Forever*
- *Career Interrupted: How 14 Successful Women Navigate Career Breaks*

Available in bookstores or
www.melbournebooks.com.au

Be part of the discussion at:

www.facebook.com/Sidewaystothetop/
www.breekthroughstrategies.com.au/publication/me-my-mentor/